Web App Testing Using Knockout.JS

Design, implement, and maintain a fully tested
JavaScript web application using Knockout.JS

Roberto Messora

PUBLISHING

BIRMINGHAM - MUMBAI

Web App Testing Using Knockout.JS

First published: November 2014

Production reference: 1101114

Published by Packt Publishing Ltd.
Livery Place
35 Livery Street
Birmingham B3 2PB, UK.

ISBN 978-1-78398-284-4

www.packtpub.com

Credits

Author
Roberto Messora

Reviewers
Paul Aldred-Bann
Oscar Finnsson
Robert Gaut
Anders Rune Jensen
Francesco Pontillo
Jon Preece

Commissioning Editor
Taron Pereira

Acquisition Editor
Subho Gupta

Content Development Editor
Arun Nadar

Technical Editor
Tanvi Bhatt

Copy Editors
Sarang Chari
Alfida Paiva
Adithi Shetty

Project Coordinator
Neha Bhatnagar

Proofreaders
Maria Gould
Robert Phillips

Indexer
Hemangini Bari

Graphics
Abhinash Sahu

Production Coordinator
Nitesh Thakur

Cover Work
Nitesh Thakur

About the Author

Roberto Messora is a product manager and software architect for geospatial IT solutions based on ESRI, Microsoft .NET, and HTML5 technology stacks. In the last few years, working as a specialist at Value Lab S.p.a. (`http://www.valuelab.it/en/`), an innovative management consulting and IT solutions company specializing in marketing, sales, and retailing, he has acquired a deep knowledge in Location Analytics and Geomarketing, delivering web applications and tools for a wide range of industries.

He also believes in an effective and collaborative team environment, adopting modern ALM techniques and tools.

I'd like to thank my wife, Adelia, and my son, Alessandro, because sometimes they don't understand very well why I spend so much time on technology and software, but they still love and support me in everything I do. I love you too. I'd like to thank my parents because a solid house needs firm foundations.

I also want to thank everyone at UGIDotNET, the biggest Italian Microsoft .NET user group, in particular Andrea Saltarello: you are an awesome developer and a remarkable friend. Isaac Newton once said: "If I have seen further, it is by standing upon the shoulders of giants."

Finally, I'd like to thank everyone involved in the production of this book, especially all my editors at Packt Publishing: Subho Gupta, Arun Nadar, and Tanvi Bhatt. Also, I really want to thank my reviewers for every suggestion that made this book better. This is my first effort on a real book, in a language that is not my mother tongue, and they held my hands from the beginning of this journey.

About the Reviewers

Paul Aldred-Bann is a full-stack .NET web developer living in Preston, England, with his wife and two children. He mainly works in C# and spends a lot of time making JavaScript bend to his object-oriented will. He's an aspiring TDDer and has discovered firsthand what "green light addiction" really is. The rest of his time is spent either with his family or recording his adventures on his blog at `aldredbann.azurewebsites.net`.

Oscar Finnsson is a software development consultant at Purepro AB, working in banking and with payment solutions. He has degrees in Engineering Physics as well as Business Administration and Economics from Uppsala University.

He is the developer behind pager.js—the most popular Knockout.JS plugin at GitHub—aimed at large, single page web applications.

Robert Gaut is a father, husband, musician, photographer, software developer, and an expert in martial arts. He started programming at the age of 12 when he wrote his first game on a Texas Instruments TI-99/4A. After receiving a degree in Music from the University of North Texas, he was invited to teach programming at a technical college. After several years of teaching, he spent more than a decade developing content management systems for the automotive industry. He currently works for a large public school district where he develops web-based applications and business workflow processes using Microsoft technologies.

Anders Rune Jensen graduated from Aalborg University in 2006, after which he quickly started his own company, IOLA. Anders has been working in the open source community for many years and is the developer of knockout.wrap.

Francesco Pontillo is a passionate software engineer who contributes to several open source projects on GitHub and likes to play with all kinds of technologies.

He currently works for a health-tech company based in Italy, where he switches from web and Android development to server-side technologies, DevOps, and data mining applications.

You can follow him on Twitter (`@frapontillo`), Google Plus (`+FrancescoPontillo`), and GitHub (`@frapontillo`).

Jon Preece is an experienced and accredited ASP.NET MVC web developer and WPF software engineer with a strong knowledge of a wide range of Microsoft technologies, especially the .NET platform. He enjoys all aspects of the software development lifecycle, and takes great pride in passing on his knowledge/skills to other people to help make them better developers. He is the lead contributor to `http://www.developerhandbook.com/`, a site dedicated to help people become better developers.

www.PacktPub.com

Support files, eBooks, discount offers, and more

You might want to visit www.PacktPub.com for support files and downloads related to your book.

Did you know that Packt offers eBook versions of every book published, with PDF and ePub files available? You can upgrade to the eBook version at www.PacktPub.com and as a print book customer, you are entitled to a discount on the eBook copy. Get in touch with us at service@packtpub.com for more details.

At www.PacktPub.com, you can also read a collection of free technical articles, sign up for a range of free newsletters and receive exclusive discounts and offers on Packt books and eBooks.

http://PacktLib.PacktPub.com

Do you need instant solutions to your IT questions? PacktLib is Packt's online digital book library. Here, you can access, read and search across Packt's entire library of books.

Why subscribe?

- Fully searchable across every book published by Packt
- Copy and paste, print and bookmark content
- On demand and accessible via web browser

Free access for Packt account holders

If you have an account with Packt at www.PacktPub.com, you can use this to access PacktLib today and view nine entirely free books. Simply use your login credentials for immediate access.

Table of Contents

Preface

This book is a starting point to meet the most important concepts and frameworks involved in modern web application production.

Delivering a web application nowadays consists of building a complete development environment, starting with a proper design and its testing, and ending with an automated build process.

Every chapter sequentially introduces a library or a tool as a specific building block of the entire environment, proposing concrete examples and development considerations: use a presentation framework with Knockout.JS, unit test in BDD style with Jasmine, design and implement a proper development strategy to achieve good unit testing coverage, and install and configure a build environment based on task automation.

This book shows a solid direction to follow when developing a web application and allows its readers to collect new hints and ideas to improve their own design strategies and delivery process.

What this book covers

Chapter 1, *Web Application Testing in the Modern Web*, is an introduction to modern web development, showing how important the testing of increasingly complex applications is. In particular, it shows how the classic client-side development based on jQuery is no longer the best solution when unit testing becomes one of the pillars of the implementation strategy. Also, it suggests that a new design approach is needed, based on a JavaScript MV presentation design pattern.

Chapter 2, The Knockout.JS UI Framework Explained, covers the most important features of Knockout.JS, which is the most well-known JavaScript presentation pattern based on Model-View-ViewModel. It also shows how to effectively use this library in a web application and why this is a good choice in terms of unit testing and application design.

Chapter 3, The Jasmine Unit Testing Framework Explained, covers the most important features of Jasmine, a very well-known JavaScript unit testing framework, based on the Behavior Driven Development approach.

Chapter 4, Unit Testing Strategies, is the core chapter of the book. It shows how to strategically deal with the development of a JavaScript web application when unit testing plays a major role. It suggests some important design principles and approaches when developing a sample web application that uses Knockout.JS as the presentation framework and Jasmine for unit testing.

Chapter 5, Setting Up an Effective Testing Environment, shows how to set up an automated testing environment based on Gulp.JS and Karma; the first is a Node.JS module that acts as a task automation system, and the second is a test runner system. It covers the steps needed to install, configure, and execute all of the system components, including unit testing reports and code coverage. It also shows how to directly test the user interface using Phantom.JS and its page automation capabilities.

What you need for this book

This book talks about web application testing. Every piece of code is written in HTML5/JavaScript/CSS3. So basically, you simply need a text editor and modern browser. In particular, the requirements are as follows:

- Jetbrains WebStorm 8 (`http://www.jetbrains.com/webstorm/download/`)
- Node.JS (`http://nodejs.org/download/`)
- Phantom.JS (`http://phantomjs.org/download.html`)
- The latest version of a web browser (Google Chrome, Mozilla Firefox, Microsoft Internet Explorer, or Apple Safari)

Who this book is for

Web App Testing Using Knockout.JS is intended for every type of JavaScript developers, from experts to beginners, who want to improve their quality standards in terms of solutions design and features correctness. Experts who already know JavaScript design patterns and unit testing can find a valid reference to put everything together in a comprehensive working framework. Beginners who barely know how to manipulate an HTML page with a multipurpose library such as jQuery can find a step-by-step introduction manual that covers all aspects of a delivery process. In general, a basic understanding of web development, HTML, and JavaScript is required.

Conventions

In this book, you will find a number of styles of text that distinguish between different kinds of information. Here are some examples of these styles, and an explanation of their meaning.

Code words in text, database table names, folder names, filenames, file extensions, pathnames, dummy URLs, user input, and Twitter handles are shown as follows: "We put the `script` tags just before the closing `body` tag for performance reasons."

A block of code is set as follows:

```
this.myModule = (function (module) {
    module.MyClass = function () {
      //MyClass definition
    }
    return module;
}(this.myModule || {}));
```

When we wish to draw your attention to a particular part of a code block, the relevant lines or items are set in bold:

```
<p>
    <span>Slider value:</span>
     
    <span id="sliderValue"></span>
     
     <button id="sliderReset">Reset</button>
</p>
```

Any command-line input or output is written as follows:

```
npm install -g gulp
```

New terms and **important words** are shown in bold. Words that you see on the screen, in menus or dialog boxes for example, appear in the text like this: "In the first one, we activate or disable the drop-down menu, whether or not the **Foreign** radio option is checked."

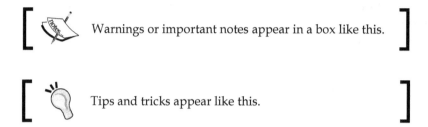

> Warnings or important notes appear in a box like this.

> Tips and tricks appear like this.

Reader feedback

Feedback from our readers is always welcome. Let us know what you think about this book—what you liked or may have disliked. Reader feedback is important for us to develop titles that you really get the most out of.

To send us general feedback, simply send an e-mail to feedback@packtpub.com, and mention the book title via the subject of your message.

If there is a topic that you have expertise in and you are interested in either writing or contributing to a book, see our author guide on www.packtpub.com/authors.

Customer support

Now that you are the proud owner of a Packt book, we have a number of things to help you to get the most from your purchase.

Downloading the example code

You can download the example code files for all Packt books you have purchased from your account at http://www.packtpub.com. If you purchased this book elsewhere, you can visit http://www.packtpub.com/support and register to have the files e-mailed directly to you.

Errata

Although we have taken every care to ensure the accuracy of our content, mistakes do happen. If you find a mistake in one of our books—maybe a mistake in the text or the code—we would be grateful if you would report this to us. By doing so, you can save other readers from frustration and help us improve subsequent versions of this book. If you find any errata, please report them by visiting http://www.packtpub.com/submit-errata, selecting your book, clicking on the **errata submission form** link, and entering the details of your errata. Once your errata are verified, your submission will be accepted and the errata will be uploaded on our website, or added to any list of existing errata, under the Errata section of that title. Any existing errata can be viewed by selecting your title from http://www.packtpub.com/support.

Piracy

Piracy of copyright material on the Internet is an ongoing problem across all media. At Packt, we take the protection of our copyright and licenses very seriously. If you come across any illegal copies of our works, in any form, on the Internet, please provide us with the location address or website name immediately so that we can pursue a remedy.

Please contact us at copyright@packtpub.com with a link to the suspected pirated material.

We appreciate your help in protecting our authors, and our ability to bring you valuable content.

Questions

You can contact us at questions@packtpub.com if you are having a problem with any aspect of the book, and we will do our best to address it.

1
Web Application Testing in the Modern Web

Every software development book tries to explain some important technical aspects of a particular framework, technology, or methodology. This book is not different from this approach, but I'd like that everyone reading these chapters will try not only to think of the technicalities, but also to keep in mind the big picture.

Yes, I'd like it very much that we, that is everyone involved in software development, really start to think about the broader scenario, at least in general terms, as the most important objective of our work.

Every technique we learn, every methodology, analysis, and nonfunctional requirement, should be treated and chosen as a brick to build a comfortable house, for a variety of reasons. Concepts such as the end users, stakeholders, project economics, and so on should be handled as primary elements when deciding to adopt a particular technology.

Throughout this book, you will learn something very important in delivering modern web applications; I hope all of these notions will be used to improve web development awareness and understanding, not personal delight.

In this chapter, you will learn:

- Why software testing should be an essential habit
- Why the classic jQuery-style development is not the best choice, unless you are developing a general purpose plugin
- Why we should consider presentation design patterns as the cornerstone of the client-side web development

Software testing

One of the most debated topics in software development is testing. There are a lot of different opinions about many aspects of software testing, from its role in the design process, to the execution frequency and codebase coverage. For example, in most of the agile methodologies, unit testing plays a primary role, but not all projects can follow a strict test-first process. We have to find the best trade-off between the development process principles and the stakeholder's environment.

Not every project is treated in the same way when we talk about software testing. From time to time, there are projects with a very low number of tests; not every part of the code base is covered by any kind of verification.

It happens, this is the real world, and it will continue to happen. However, this is not a healthy way to proceed. Basically, software testing is the proper way to prove that our solution:

- Works as expected
- Meets functional and nonfunctional requirements
- Is free of defects

There are contracts that consider that a project has concluded only in the presence of the appropriate documentation showing the correct system operation. To reach this objective, we need a solid testing strategy; this means that we need to carefully choose the following:

- The right testing levels (unit, integration, acceptance, and so on)
- The right testing types (regression, acceptance, usability, security, and so on)
- The right testing process (test first, waterfall, top-down, and so on)
- The right testing tools (frameworks, third-party products, dedicated environments, and so on)
- The right testing outputs/reports, depending on who will evaluate them

Every single topic in these bullet points carries years of professional experience; it's not easy and immediate to become an expert. I also have to say that not every project covers all the enlisted items because of budget, time, or team habits.

On the other hand, there are two main reasons that suggest introducing at least a basic testing coverage from the bottom:

- Better design
- To avoid regression errors

This is a minimal scenario, but it's important to define a starting point, and I think this is the best place to begin a journey that will lead to a new way to consider software development.

This starting point is called **unit testing**, the first level of software testing; it works directly on the code and is usually the easiest to set up and learn.

This kind of testing should never be absent in any software solution. There are plenty of frameworks and libraries for the most important programming languages and **Integrated Development Environments** (IDEs); not writing tests is just a matter of will.

This book talks about web application testing, but it's not intended to be an exhaustive reference for software testing; more of a short manual, so we need to focus on unit testing. However, it's very important to understand that you should consider this book in a broader context, a piece in the jigsaw.

In particular, this is not a book that talks about **Test Driven Development** (TDD). TDD is a design methodology that leverages unit testing as the primary working tool. It's quite common to use TDD and unit testing as synonyms, but this is not correct. You cannot practice TDD without unit testing, but you can write unit tests without TDD and improve your design anyway.

In this book, I'd like to show what you need to do to set up a proper testing environment for a web solution, not teach you how to design your applications. Software design is a question of professional experience and involves a lot of general development aspects not specifically related to web development. On the other hand, what you will learn in this book is strictly related to the web application scenario, because we will talk about technical details, frameworks, and libraries that you can only find in web development.

By the way, you are welcome to apply TDD in web development using what you find in these chapters.

The modern Web

The Web has changed a lot since HTML5 made its appearance. We are witnessing a gradual shift from a classic full server-side web development to a new architectural asset that moves much of the application logic to the client side.

The general objective is to deliver **rich internet applications** (RIA) with a desktop-like user experience. Think about web applications such as Gmail or Facebook. If you maximize your browser, they look like full desktop applications in terms of usability, UI effects, responsiveness, and richness.

Usually, solution architecture is quite simple, a rich and complex user interface on the client side, some application services on the server side. The technology scenario is also very straightforward. On the client side, HTML5, JavaScript, and CSS3 are the emerging options. They are replacing older plugin technologies such as Adobe Flash and Microsoft Silverlight. On the server side, **HTTP RESTful** services are widely adopted because of their implementation simplicity and standardization across a large variety of programming languages.

This is the main technology trend. Maybe it's not the best technological choice, but it has many advantages in terms of simplicity, integration, and user device penetration.

Widespread device diffusion is undoubtedly one of the most important key success factors of the magic trio, HTML5, JavaScript, and CSS3. In fact, we can assert that almost every device with a modern web browser (PC, tablet, or smartphone) is able to access and deliver an HTML5 application to the user.

In other words, this is why we are here. There are millions of devices out there that allow end users to access our web applications, and we need to assure a reliable interaction for them. Think about home banking web sites. If you access your bank account, you won't feel very comfortable if a money transfer fails because of an application defect. Maybe because developers forgot a critical data validation or didn't properly handle a remote service error, you don't know if your transfer has been accepted or not.

Web applications are growing in complexity, not just because of modern web technologies, but also because of marketing strategies, product placements, or simple market competition. In this scenario, tightly related to the visibility and reputation of a company, we cannot approve a delivery plan that doesn't provide some kind of testing strategy.

Once we establish that testing is a pillar of our solution, we need to understand which is the best way to proceed in terms of software architecture and development. In this regard, it's very important to determine the very basic design principles that allow a proper approach to unit testing. In fact, even though HTML5 is a recent achievement, HTML and JavaScript are technologies that have been in use for quite some time.

The problem here is that many developers tend to approach modern web development in the same old way. This is a grave mistake because back in time, client-side JavaScript development was a underrated and mostly confined to simple UI graphic management.

Client-side development is historically driven by libraries such as **Prototype**, **jQuery**, and **Dojo**, whose primary feature is **DOM** (HTML Document Object Model or HTML markup) management. They can work in small web applications, but as soon as these grow in complexity, the codebase starts to become unmanageable and unmaintainable. We can't think that we can continue to develop JavaScript in the same way we did 10 years ago. In those days, we only had to apply some of the UI transformations dynamically. Today, we have to deliver full working applications.

We need a better design, but most of all we need to reconsider the client-side JavaScript development and apply the advanced design patterns and principles.

Coming back to the context of this book, a new development approach is essential if one of our objectives is a testable codebase. In fact, once we decide that we want to test our solution, we need to write testable code.

Does this sound silly? Well… not at all. We can't simply say that we want to test our code. We must ensure that it is possible. Not all code is testable.

Roy Osherove in his book, *The Art of Unit Testing*, gives the following definition:

> *"A unit test is a piece of a code (usually a method) that invokes another piece of code and checks the correctness of some assumptions afterward. If the assumptions turn out to be wrong, the unit test has failed. A unit is a method or function."*

Martin Fowler also writes about unit testing and the concept of **isolation** (`http://martinfowler.com/bliki/UnitTest.html`):

> *"A more important distinction is whether the unit you're testing should be isolated from its collaborators. Imagine you're testing an order class's price method. The price method needs to invoke some functions on the product and customer classes. If you follow the principle of collaborator isolation you don't want to use the real product or customer classes here, because a fault in the customer class would cause the order class's tests to fail. Instead you use TestDoubles for the collaborators."*

These definitions of unit testing talk about code that verifies other code isolating individual parts of a program. It's clear that we need to provide at least these basic characteristics to our code if we want to test it. In this book, we are going to suggest some useful design principles, but we won't focus on software development methodologies (for example, Extreme Programming, Waterfall, Agile, and others).

Escaping from the jQuery-style development

The World Wide Web is a fairly simple environment; all the content available is accessible using a web browser. Also, web browsers are conceptually simple applications. They ask for a web resource, a server sends that resource, and they display what's inside the received data. A web resource is nothing else than a series of files that represents different types of content:

- **User interface structures**: HTML markup
- **User interface graphic styles**: CSS
- **User interface programs and executables**: JavaScript
- **Data**: JSON or XML

Every browser supports these four types of content even if there are some interpretation differences (global standardization has not yet been reached).

We can say that JavaScript is the programming language of the Web, but its native DOM API is somewhat rudimentary. We have to write a lot of code to manage and transform HTML markup to bring the UI to life with some dynamic user interaction. Also, full standardization does not mean that the same code will work differently (or work at all) in different browsers.

Over the past few years, developers decided to resolve this situation; JavaScript libraries such as Prototype, jQuery, and Dojo have come to light.

jQuery is one of the most known open source JavaScript libraries, published in 2006 for the first time. Its huge success is mainly due to the following reasons:

- A simple and detailed API that allows us to manage HTML DOM elements
- Cross-browser support
- Simple and effective extensibility

Since its appearance, it has been used by thousands of developers as the foundation library. A large amount of JavaScript code all around the world has been built with jQuery in mind. A jQuery ecosystem grew up very quickly, and nowadays there are plenty of jQuery plugins that implement virtually everything related to web development.

A typical jQuery-based web application is something like the following sample page:

```html
<!DOCTYPE html>
<html>
<head lang="en">
    <meta charset="UTF-8">
    <title>jQuery Sample</title>
    <style type="text/css">
        ...
    </style>
</head>
<body>
    <h4>jQuery Sample</h4>
    <form id="inputForm">
        <label for="firstName">Name: </label>
        <br>
        <input type="text" id="firstName" name="firstName">
        <br>
        <label for="lastName">Last Name: </label>
        <br>
        <input type="text" id="lastName" name="lastName">
        <br>
        <fieldset>
            <legend>Nationality:</legend>
            <input type="radio" name="nat" value="it" checked>Italian
            <br>
            <input type="radio" name="nat" value="foreign">Foreign
            <br>
            <select id="foreignNat" disabled="disabled">
                <option value="">Select an item...</option>
                <option value="us">American</option>
                <option value="uk">British</option>
                <option value="fr">French</option>
                <option value="other">Other</option>
            </select>
        </fieldset>
        <input type="submit" value="Submit">
        <br>
        <p id="resultMessage"></p>c
    </form>
    <script type="text/JavaScript" src="//ajax.googleapis.com/ajax/
libs/jquery/1.11.0/jquery.min.js"></script>
    <script type="text/JavaScript">
        //JavaScript Code
    </script>
</body>
</html>
```

This is a simple HTML page with a single form and bunch of inputs:

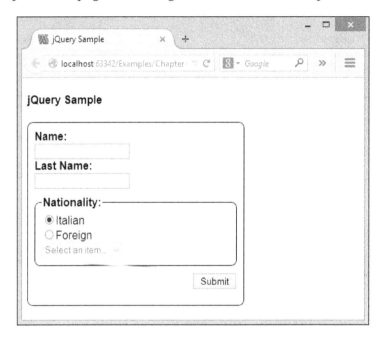

If we want to validate this form before submission, we can add the following code in the script tag:

```
function showMessage (message, isError) {
  jQuery("#resultMessage").text(message);
  if (isError) {
    jQuery("#resultMessage").css("color", "red");
  } else {
    jQuery("#resultMessage").css("color", "green");
  }
  jQuery("#resultMessage").css("visibility", "visible");
}
```

```
function hideMessage () {
  jQuery("#resultMessage").css("visibility", "hidden");
}

hideMessage();

jQuery(document).ready(function () {
  jQuery("#inputForm input:radio").on("click", function () {
    if (jQuery(this).val() === "it") {
      jQuery("#foreignNat option").removeAttr("selected");
      jQuery("#foreignNat").attr("disabled", "disabled");
    } else {
      jQuery("#foreignNat").removeAttr("disabled");
    }
  });
  jQuery("form").submit(function (e) {
    e.preventDefault();
    hideMessage();
    jQuery("#resultMessage").text("Please fill First Name");
    if (!jQuery("#firstName").val()) {
      showMessage("Please fill First Name", true);
      return;
    }
    if (!jQuery("#lastName").val()) {
      showMessage("Please fill Last Name", true);
      return;
    }
    if (!jQuery("input[name=nat]:checked").val()) {
      showMessage("Please select Nationality", true);
      return;
    }
    if ((jQuery("input[name=nat]:checked").val() === "foreign") &&
      (!jQuery("#foreignNat option:selected").val())){
      showMessage("Please select Foreign Nationality", true);
      return;
    }
    //form submission, for example with an AJAX call
    showMessage("Form submitted", false);
  });
});
```

The preceding code is a typical example of jQuery-style programming. Nearly every line contains a jQuery call, from pure tag content management to event handling. It works and is also a simple API to learn; an average developer becomes productive in a very short period of time.

In the preceding code, we defined two helper functions (`showMessage` and `hideMessage`) to show and hide the alert message. Then, when the page is fully loaded (`jQuery(document).ready(...)`), we defined two event handler functions: one for the radio button click (`jQuery("#inputForm input:radio").on("click",` `...)`) and the other for the form submission (`jQuery("form").submit(...)`).

In the first one, we activate or disable the drop-down menu, whether or not the **Foreign** radio option is checked:

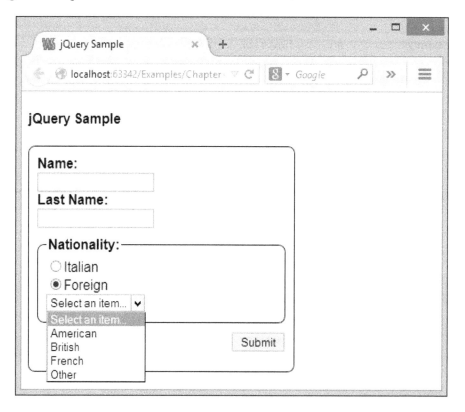

In the second event handler function, we make some input validation and proceed with form submission only if all the inputs are properly filled, providing a specific status message.

The preceding example is a simple one: there are a few HTML tags, the UI logic is quite simple (just a message that appears/disappears and drop-down menu that activates/deactivates), and the validation is pretty straightforward.

Yet, despite its simplicity, all of the code that we just wrote is virtually untestable. There are two main reasons:

- User interface items are tightly coupled with the user interface logic
- The user interface logic spans inside the event handler callback functions

The real problem here is that everything passes through a jQuery reference, that is, a `jQuery("something")` call. This means that we always need a live reference of the HTML page, otherwise those calls fail, and this is also true for a unit test case. We can't think of testing a piece of user interface logic running an entire web application!

Consider a real-case scenario, not this super simple example of a complex e-commerce website, and we need to test a specific page. We need to reach this page first (maybe we also need to enter some user credentials because it's a private page), provide some input data, and then start our test case. Think of repeating this journey as many times as different input data combinations are possible, or try to automate this process in someway. A real nightmare!

Worse than this, you have to repeat the entire process if you simply change a single HTML tag ID and nothing else. The UI logic is unchanged, but we need to assure that no jQuery tag reference breaks if we change something in the HTML markup. This is really too much work to do. We will soon realize that we spend more time running unit tests than developing the application.

On the other hand, large jQuery applications tend to be monolithic because jQuery itself allows the callback function nesting very easily and doesn't really promote any particular design strategy. The result is often a spaghetti code.

jQuery is a good option if you want to develop a specific custom plugin. We will also continue to use this library for pure user interface effects and animations, but we need something different to maintain a large web application's logic.

Presentation design patterns

In the previous section, you learned that a development approach based on jQuery is not a good idea for a large web application.

To move a step forward, we need to decide what's the best option in terms of testable code. The main topic here is the application design; in other words, how we can build our codebase following a general guideline with testability in mind.

In software engineering, there's nothing better than not reinventing the wheel; we can rely on a safe and reliable resource: design patterns. Wikipedia provides a good definition for the term *design pattern* (`http://en.wikipedia.org/wiki/Software_design_pattern`):

> *"In software engineering, a design pattern is a general reusable solution to a commonly occurring problem within a given context in software design.*
>
> *A design pattern is not a finished design that can be transformed directly into source or machine code. It is a description or template for how to solve a problem that can be used in many different situations.*
>
> *Patterns are formalized best practices that the programmer can use to solve common problems when designing an application or system."*

There are tons of specific design patterns, but we also need something related to the presentation layer because this is where a JavaScript web application belongs.

The most important aspect in terms of design and maintainability of a JavaScript web application is a clear separation between the user interface (basically, the HTML markup) and the presentation logic (the JavaScript code that turns a web page dynamic and responsive to user interaction). This is what you learned digging into a typical jQuery web application.

According to MSDN's *patterns & practices*, there are other important aspects involved in the presentation design patterns (`http://msdn.microsoft.com/en-us/library/ff647343.aspx`):

- Document simple mechanisms that work
- Provide a common vocabulary and taxonomy for developers and architects
- Enable solutions to be described concisely as combinations of patterns
- Enable the reuse of architecture, design, and implementation decisions
- You have to support user interactions of increasing complexity, involving complex relationships between forms and pages in the user interface
- Existing business processes change and you have to present new or modified functionalities to your users
- You have to port your application to other platforms or make the application accessible to additional client types (such as mobile devices)

At this point, we need to identify an effective implementation of a presentation design pattern and use it in our web applications. In this regard, I have to admit that the JavaScript community has made an extraordinary job in the last two years. So far, there are tons of frameworks and libraries that implement a particular presentation design pattern.

We only need to choose which framework fits our needs, for example, we can start by taking a look at the MyTodo MVC website (`http://todomvc.com/`). This is an open source project that shows how to build the same web application using a different library each time.

In this book, we will use **Knockout.JS**, one of the most popular libraries that implements the **Model-View-ViewModel** design pattern.

Most of these libraries implement a so-called **MV*** design pattern (Knockout.JS does this too). MV* means that every design pattern belongs to a broader family with a common root, which is **Model-View-Controller**. The MVC pattern is one of the oldest and most enduring architectural design patterns. Originally designed by Trygve Reenskaug, working on Smalltalk-80 back in 1979, it has been heavily refactored since then.

Basically, the MVC pattern enforces the isolation of business data (**Models**) from user interfaces (**Views**), with a third component (**Controllers**) managing the logic and user input. It can be described as (*Addy Osmani, Learning JavaScript Design Patterns*, `http://addyosmani.com/resources/essentialjsdesignpatterns/book/#detailmvc`):

- A Model representing domain-specific data and ignorant of the user interface (Views and Controllers). When a model is changed, it will inform its observers.

- A View representing the current state of a Model. The *Observer pattern* was used to let the View know whenever the Model was updated or modified.

- Presentation was taken care of by the View, but there wasn't just a single View and Controller — a View-Controller pair was required for each section or element being displayed on the screen.

- The Controller's role in this pair handles user interaction (such as key-presses and actions, for example, clicks), making decisions for the View.

This general definition has slightly changed over the years, not only to adapt its implementation to different technologies and programming languages, but also because changes have been made to the Controller part. **Model-View-Presenter** and **Model-View-ViewModel** are the most well known alternatives to the MVC pattern.

The MV* presentation design patterns are a valid answer to our need; an architectural design guideline that promotes separation of concerns and isolation, the two most important factors needed for software testing. In this way, we can test the models, views, and third actor whatever it is (a Controller, Presenter, ViewModel, and so on) separately.

On the other hand, adopting a presentation design pattern doesn't mean that we cease to use jQuery. jQuery is a great library and we will continue to add its reference to our pages, but we will also integrate its use wisely in a better design context.

Summary

This chapter gives a significant vision about software testing in the contemporary web era, starting with the most important consideration; it's unimaginable to think of a web application that is not supported by a solid testing strategy.

You learned that modern web development can't follow the same old paradigms such as using the well known jQuery library as the application cornerstone. Complex web applications tend to become unmanageable and untestable without a good architectural design. Every framework or library should be used in the correct context. jQuery has advantages in developing a plugin and pure user interface customizations, but it's not the best option if adopted as an application logic framework.

We finally saw that if we want to satisfy both maintainability and testability, we need to adopt a presentation design pattern. In the JavaScript community, the emerging presentation frameworks and libraries are a part of the MV* family and they promote separation of concerns and isolation between their components. In particular, Knockout.JS is one of the most well-known libraries and implements a specific pattern variation, which is Model-View-ViewModel.

In the next chapter, you will learn more about Knockout.JS and its features.

2
The Knockout.JS UI Framework Explained

One of the two main topics of this book is **Knockout.JS**, a JavaScript library that simplifies the development process of rich and dynamic user interfaces. Knockout.JS is one of many libraries out there that implements a presentation design pattern, in particular the **Model-View-ViewModel** (**MVVM**).

We will review Version 3.1 and its most important concepts and features using several examples, and try to understand why this library is so important in relation to testing a web application.

However, this book is not intended to be a complete Knockout.JS compendium; please refer to the Knockout.JS website documentation (`http://knockoutjs.com/documentation/introduction.html`) to discover all the advanced topics and references that are not covered in this chapter.

In this chapter, you will learn:

- How to introduce and use Knockout.JS in a web application
- The data bind mechanism that turns a web application dynamic
- How Knockout.JS promotes a clear separation between the JavaScript code and HTML markup and why this is a good practice for testing

Hello Knockout.JS

To start using Knockout.JS is very simple. It is nothing more than a couple of JavaScript lines of code and a special attribute added to the DOM tags.

An example of an HTML page can be as follows:

```html
<!DOCTYPE html>
<html>
<head lang="en">
    <meta charset="UTF-8">
    <title>Hello Knockout.JS</title>
</head>
<body>
    <span data-bind="text: message"></span>
    <script type="text/javascript" src="http://cdnjs.cloudflare.com/ajax/libs/knockout/3.1.0/knockout-min.js"></script>
    <script type="text/JavaScript">
        var viewModel = {
            message: "Hello Knockout.JS!"
        };
        ko.applyBindings(viewModel);
    </script>
</body>
</html>
```

We put the `script` tags just before the closing `body` tag for performance reasons, as stated in the best practices document of the Yahoo Developer Network (`https://developer.yahoo.com/performance/rules.html#js_bottom`), but also because DOM is fully loaded before the execution.

Here's the page that is loaded into a browser:

Analyzing the page source, we can find:

- A special `data-bind` attribute declared in the `span` tag
- A `script` tag that references the Knockout.JS library from a well-known **Content Delivery Network (CDN)**
- A JavaScript object called `viewModel` with a single `message` property
- A method invocation to `ko.applyBindings`

> Knockout.JS leverages one of the new HTML5 features: **custom data attributes**. Most commonly known as **data dash attributes**, they are defined by W3C as *intended to store custom data private to the page or application, for which there are no more appropriate attributes or elements* (`http://www.w3.org/TR/2010/WD-html5-20101019/elements.html#custom-data-attribute`).
>
> The Knockout.JS convention is to use the word *bind* after the default *data-* suffix.

Despite the simplicity of the preceding example, we can depict a typical Knockout.JS development process anyway:

1. The first step is placing a reference to the Knockout.JS library. We used a `script` tag that points to CDNJS (`http://cdnjs.com/`), one of the most important CDNs, as suggested on the Knockout.JS website (`http://knockoutjs.com/downloads/index.html`).

2. The second step is creating a JavaScript object, the **VideModel**, with some properties; this object is basically a container for data to be shown on the web page (the **Model**). We used a simple literal object called `viewModel` with a single `message` string property.

3. The third step is adding some HTML tags to the page (the **View**) that will work as placeholders for the ViewModel data. Then, add a particular attribute called `data-bind`. The value of this attribute follows a specific syntax that in the simplest form is `<binding type>: <ViewModel property>`. It declares that the ViewModel property is linked to the containing DOM tag in a way specified by the data-bind type. We used a `span` tag and the `text` binding type linked to the ViewModel `message` property.

4. The fourth step is invoking the ko.applyBindings method passing the ViewModel object as a parameter. The ko object is the main Knockout.JS object and it's available once the library is fully loaded. The applyBindings method is the method that does the magic and activates the whole Knockout.JS mechanism; it scans the HTML document for data-bind attributes, decodes the attribute values, and reacts accordingly. In the example provided, it finds that the message ViewModel property is linked to the span tag through the text binding. It then inserts the message value inside the span opening and closing tags.

If we analyze the HTML **Document Object Model (DOM)** at runtime with a browser developer tool, we get the following final result:

```
<span data-bind="text: message">Hello Knockout.JS!</span>
```

The ko.applyBindings method has two versions: ko.applyBindings(viewModel), which implicitly considers the body tag as the root element and applies data-binding to the entire page, and ko.applyBindings(viewModel, document. getElementById("elementID")), which considers the elementID tag as the root element and applies data-binding to all its children. This means that in a single HTML page, Knockout.JS can provide multiple views defined by different markup fragments, all of which need a call to the ko.applyBindings method.

The web page is up and running, everything works as expected, but it's static. If any modification to the message property occur, nothing will happen to the page. To make the page dynamic, we need something more.

Automatic synchronization between View and ViewModel

In the previous section, we saw a simple example. Now we need to go further to introduce some new concepts. The following example refines the first one:

```
<!DOCTYPE html>
<html>
<head lang="en">
    <meta charset="UTF-8">
    <title>Hello Knockout.JS</title>
</head>
<body>
```

```html
<span>Type a message: </span>
<input type="text" data-bind="value: message" />
<button data-bind="click: submitMessage">Click me</button>
<script type="text/javascript" src="http://cdnjs.cloudflare.com/
ajax/libs/knockout/3.1.0/knockout-min.js"></script>
<script type="text/JavaScript">
    var ViewModel = function () {
        this.message = ko.observable("");
        this.submitMessage= function () {
            alert(this.message());
        };
    };
    var viewModel = new ViewModel();
    ko.applyBindings(viewModel);
</script>
</body>
</html>
```

Once we run the page, we can type a message inside the textbox and then click on the **Click me** button; the browser will show the same text-box message:

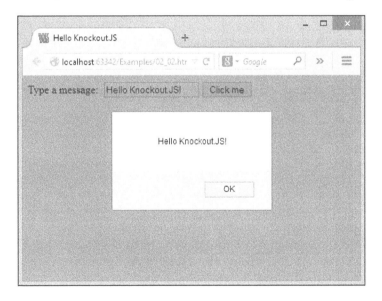

We made some changes to the previous example:

- The ViewModel is now declared as a class:
    - The `message` property is no longer defined as a simple string but initialized by invoking the `ko.observable` method
    - There is a `submitMessage` method that shows the user the value of `message`

- The `data-bind` attribute linked to the `message` property is now declared inside the `input` tag and its type is `value`

- Another `data-bind` attribute is declared in a button tag; it's linked to the `submitMessage` method and its type is `click`

There is something particular about the `message` property. We initialized the property using a special Knockout.JS method, `ko.observable`, providing an empty string. However, when we recall its value in the `submitMessage` method, we used a method invocation syntax using parenthesis. Actually, the `message` property is not a real property, technically speaking, it's a method, but we use it as a data container so that we can consider it as a ViewModel property. The reason resides in the `ko.observable` method; it creates a special object called **observable**. The parameter is the initial value. Once the observable object is created, we can set its value calling the object as a method and passing the new value. When we want to retrieve its value, we call it in the same way but without any parameter:

```
var myProperty = ko.observable(3); //intialization
alert(myProperty()); //it shows 3
myProperty(5); //setting a new value
alert(myProperty()); //it shows 5
```

What is very important here is why we use an observable object to create a ViewModel property. Observable means that this kind of object can automatically notify its state modifications to anyone that subscribes to the event. In Knockout.JS, when a ViewModel property is linked to a View `data-bind` attribute, the framework creates a bidirectional state modification subscription. When the ViewModel property changes, it also automatically changes the tag content (accordingly to the data-bind type), and vice versa.

Returning to our example, when we type a message inside the textbox, we are changing the `input` tag value. This is linked to the ViewModel `message` property through the `data-bind` attribute of type `value`. The `message` property is modified with the same value we typed. When we click on the **Click me** button, the browser shows the same string we typed using the `message` property.

Another important point is how Knockout.JS manages the View events. When the user clicks on the button, the click event is handled with a click binding that is linked to a ViewModel method. This means that the data-binding mechanism is not only referred to data, but also to **commands**: ViewModel methods that handle View events triggered by the user.

This mechanism depicts the automatic synchronization from the View to the ViewModel, but the nature of this link is bidirectional; let's take a look at a little modification to the example:

```
<!DOCTYPE html>
<html>
<head lang="en">
    <meta charset="UTF-8">
    <title>Hello Knockout.JS</title>
</head>
<body>
<span>Type a message: </span>
<input type="text" data-bind="value: message" />
<button data-bind="click: submitMessage">Click me</button>
<br />
<span data-bind="text: summary"></span>
<script type="text/javascript" src="http://cdnjs.cloudflare.com/ajax/
libs/knockout/3.1.0/knockout-min.js"></script>
<script type="text/JavaScript">
    var ViewModel = function () {
        this.message = ko.observable("");
        this.summary = ko.observable("");
        this.submitMessage = function () {
            this.summary("You typed: " + this.message());
        };
    };
    var viewModel = new ViewModel();
    ko.applyBindings(viewModel);
</script>
</body>
</html>
```

Once we run the page, we can type a message inside the textbox, and then, click on the **Click me** button, the content of the span tag will be updated:

We introduced a new ViewModel summary property, which is modified inside the submitMessage method using the message property value. We linked this property to a new span tag using a text binding.

This new example demonstrates that if we change the value of an observable inside the code, the data-binding mechanism also works from the ViewModel to the View; the span tag content changes simply when the ViewModel property linked to it is modified.

At this point, we can summarize the most important concepts of Knockout.JS:

- An HTML fragment (or an entire page) is considered as a View

- A View is always associated to a JavaScript object called ViewModel; this is a code representation of the View that contains the data (Model) to show (in the form of properties) and the commands that handle View events triggered by the user (in the form of methods)

- The association between View and ViewModel is built around the concept of data-binding, a mechanism that provides automatic bidirectional synchronization:

  ° In the View, the data-binding is declared placing the data-bind attributes into the DOM elements. The attributes' values must follow a specific syntax that specifies the nature of the association and target ViewModel property/method.

○ In the ViewModel, methods are considered as commands, and properties are defined as special objects called observables. The observables main feature is the capability to notify every state modification.

The ViewModel in detail

A ViewModel is a pure-code representation of the View. We saw in the previous sections that it contains data to show and commands that handle events triggered by the user.

It's important to remember that a ViewModel shouldn't have any knowledge about the View and the UI. Pure-code representation means that a ViewModel shouldn't contain any reference to HTML markup elements (buttons, text-boxes, and so on.) but only pure JavaScript properties and methods.

Knockout.JS is a JavaScript implementation of the Model-View-ViewModel presentation design pattern whose objective is to promote a clear separation between the View and ViewModel. This principle is called **Separation of Concerns**.

Why is this so important? The answer is quite easy, because in this way a developer can achieve a real separation of responsibilities. The View is only responsible for presenting data to the user and reacting to her/his inputs. The ViewModel is also responsible for holding the data and providing the presentation logic.

The following diagram from Microsoft MSDN depicts the existing relationships between the three pattern actors very well (http://msdn.microsoft.com/en-us/library/ff798384.aspx):

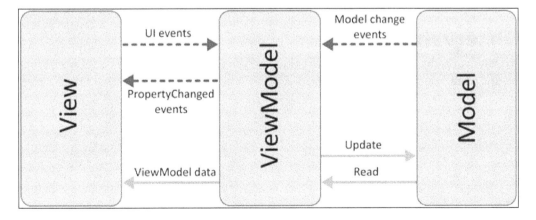

Thinking about a web application in these terms leads to ViewModel development without any reference to the DOM element's IDs or any other markup-related code, as in the classic jQuery style. There are two main reasons behind this:

- As the web application becomes more complex, the number of DOM elements increases and it's not uncommon to reach a point in which it becomes very difficult to manage all the IDs with the typical jQuery-fluent interface style. The JavaScript codebase very soon turns into a spaghetti code nightmare.

- A clear separation between the View and ViewModel allows a new way of working. JavaScript developers can concentrate on the presentation logic; UX experts on the other hand, can provide HTML markup focusing on user interaction and how the web application will look. The two groups can work quite independently and agree on basic contact points using the `data-bind` tag attributes.

The key feature of a ViewModel is the observable object; a special object capable to notify its state modifications to any subscribers. There are three types of observable objects:

- The basic observable object based on JavaScript data types (string, number, and so on)

- The **computed observable** dependent on other observables or computed observables

- The **observable array**, which is a standard JavaScript array with a built-in change notification mechanism

In the following sections, we will review the most important key feature of these objects.

Observables

We have already talked about observables, so we won't repeat the basic concepts around their use in a ViewModel.

However, there is an interesting feature that sometimes is very useful, manual explicit subscription. The data-binding mechanism creates an automatic implicit subscription to observable state modification, but it's possible to manually subscribe to the same event:

```
var ViewModel = function () {
  this.message = ko.observable("Hello Knockout.JS!");
};
var viewModel = new ViewModel();
var subscription = viewModel.message.subscribe(function(newValue) {
  alert("The new message is: " + newValue);
};
```

In this example, we used the `subscribe` method passing a callback function that will be invoked every time the `message` observable will change its value. The new value is provided as an argument.

Please refer to the Knockout.JS website to discover advanced topics such as extenders; a way to augment an observable object adding custom features and properties (`http://knockoutjs.com/documentation/extenders.html`).

Computed observables

A computed observable is an observable object that commonly depends on other observables or computed observables. This dependency is defined by a function that returns a combination of the original observables' values.

A computed observable is commonly used as a ViewModel read-only property:

```
var PersonViewModel = function () {
  var self = this;
  self.firstName = ko.observable("Roberto");
  self.lastName = ko.observable("Messora");
  self.age = ko.observable(41);
  self.fullName = ko.computed(function () {
    return self.firstName() + " " + self.lastName();
  });
  self.completeInfo = ko.computed(function () {
    return self.fullName() + " (" + self.age() + ")";
  });
};
```

The `var self = this` expression as a starting expression is a typical JavaScript idiom needed to store the `this` context object in a private variable, for later use. This idiomatic expression is widely adopted because JavaScript is a language in which the context object binding is not implicit as in C# or Java. Without the `self` variable, we should write a computed observable specifying the `this` context object:

```
this.myComputed = ko.computed(function () {
    return this.myFirstObservable() + " - " + this.
mySecondObservable();
}, this);
```

I suggest digging into this concept to understand this fundamental JavaScript feature.

The preceding example reports a ViewModel with three observable (`firstName`, `lastName`, and `age`) and two computed observable (`fullName` and `completeInfo`) properties.

The `fullName` computed observable is a combination of the `firstName` and `lastName` observables. The `completeInfo` computed observable is a combination of the `fullName` computed observable and the `age` observable.

A computed observable is an observable object; it has to notify its state modifications but it doesn't store any value. It's a combination of other observables. How is this possible? The **automatic dependency tracking** mechanism behind a computed observable triggers the function evaluation every time any one of the dependent observables changes its value. This means, for example, that if `firstName` changes its value, both `fullName` and `completeInfo` trigger their state modification re-evaluating their definition function because `fullName` depends directly on `firstName`, and `completeInfo` depends on `fullName`.

A computed observable can be writable, this is an advanced topic, but it can be a useful solution in those rare cases, such as user input decomposition, value converters, user input filtering, and validation (`http://knockoutjs.com/documentation/computed-writable.html`).

Observable arrays

One of the most used data structures is collections. They are everywhere in web applications and Knockout.JS offers a special version of a JavaScript array called the observable array.

An observable array behaves like a regular array but also provides a set of new features that allows managing a list of elements inside a ViewModel. The most important feature is the capability of tracking the elements in the array. An observable array triggers its state modification when an element is added, removed, or the array itself is reordered.

What's important here is that an observable array tracks the collection modifications, not the internal state of its elements. If an element changes its value or a property value, the observable array doesn't notify anything. On the other hand, nothing prevents us from using minimal ViewModels as elements (with minimal ViewModel, I mean objects that use observables for properties).

To create and use an observable array is very straightforward:

```
var ViewModel = function () {
  this.numbers = ko.observableArray(); //empty observable array
  this.users = ko.observableArray([
    {
      name: "Roberto Messora"
    }, {
      name: "Jim T. Kirk"
    }
  ]); //observable array with two literal objects
};
...
var viewModel = new ViewModel();
viewModel.numbers.push(3); //adds an element
alert(viewModel.numbers()[0]); //shows 3
alert(viewModel.users().length); //shows 2
```

The preceding example shows two aspects:

- We can call a common array method such as push through the observable array directly; this is true for all the common array methods (push, pop, slice, and so on). An observable array redefines all of them for better performance and state tracking.

- Prior to accessing the first element of the collection, we have to recall the regular array behind the observable, invoking the observable array property as a method (using parenthesis). This is also true for every regular array property such as length.

Finally, an observable array adds a bunch of new methods that are not present in a regular array, such as remove, removeAll, destroy, and destroyAll.

Data-binding in detail

The main objective of a web application is to present some data and eventually react to user inputs. In the previous sections, you learned that the Model-View-ViewModel strategy is to hold the data (the Model) and commands in a pure-code representation of the View called ViewModel. We also briefly scratched the surface of the data-binding mechanism that permits the connection between the ViewModel and HTML markup.

In this section, we will review the Knockout.JS built-in data-binding types. There are many ways to present information on a web page. There are plenty of elements in HTML that need a way to bind the ViewModel properties and commands.

The data-binding syntax

In Knockout.JS, we talk about declarative data-binding because we need to place the data-bind attributes inside the HTML tags, and specify what kind of binding is associated to a ViewModel property/command.

The attribute value must follow a specific syntax in order to allow Knockout.JS to decode its content during the applyBindings method. The correct syntax is a sequence of elements separated by commas. Every element is a name/value pair separated by a colon. The name is a data-binding identifier and the value is one of the following:

- A ViewModel property (static or observable)
- A ViewModel method (a command)
- A JavaScript conditional expression
- An inline JavaScript function
- A JavaScript literal object (some bindings need an object with several properties to declare their configuration)

Obviously if a data-bind attribute value is malformed or one of the name/value pairs is not recognized (wrong name and/or value), Knockout.JS notifies an exception.

The following are examples of the data-binding syntax:

```
<span data-bind="text: message, visible: isVisible></span>
<input type="button" data-bind="click: submitData" value="Submit" />
<span data-bind="text: elementCount, visible: myArray().length > 0"></span>
<span data-bind="text: username || 'Anonymous'" ></span>
```

The third and forth rows depict how we can introduce inline or conditional expressions in a data-bind attribute.

Please be very careful not to misuse the inline functions. The fact that it is permitted doesn't mean we should place whichever JavaScript expression we can think about. Remember that in Model-View-ViewModel, a ViewModel's responsibility is to hold the presentation logic. In case of uncertainty, it's far better to create a new ViewModel property than write an inline expression in a data-bind attribute. Keep inline expressions very simple, not only because it's a design pattern principle, but also because they are strings inside HTML markup. The more complex they are, the higher the probability to introduce JavaScript syntax errors, also it's very hard to read inside the HTML markup.

In the following sections, we will briefly review all the built-in Knockout.JS bindings. Please refer to the project website documentation for detailed information about the specific syntax used in every binding type. There are many detailed options and variants. This book is not intended to be a reference manual, but I think it's important to understand all the available configurations.

Text and appearance bindings

The simplest type of data-binding is the one that has something to do with text and appearance. Knockout.JS defines the following built-in bindings:

- `text`: This represents the text inside a DOM element, usually a string inside the opening and closing tag
- `html`: This represents the inner HTML markup inside a DOM element (be careful with this binding because of malicious script injection attempts)
- `style`: This controls the `style` attribute of a DOM element
- `css`: This allows adding or removing CSS classes in a DOM element
- `attr`: This controls the value of a valid chosen attribute of a DOM element
- `visible`: This controls the visibility style of a DOM element using a Boolean value (the element is always present inside the page, hidden or visible)

Conditional and loop bindings

Knockout.JS provides a set of bindings that control how and when an HTML markup fragment is present inside the whole page source. They are:

- `foreach`: This repeats a DOM element as many times as the number of elements inside an array. Typically, it's used in combination with an observable array to visualize lists or tables (every DOM element is bound to an element of the array).

- `if`: This controls the presence of a DOM element inside the page using a Boolean value. It differs from the `visible` binding, because if the values is `false`, the element is not physically present in the HTML page nor simply hidden. Also, data-bindings of descendants are not applied when the `if` binding evaluates to `false`.

- `ifnot`: This is the inverted version of the `if` binding.

- `with`: This is conceptually similar to the `with` statement of Visual Basic. It allows you to change the current binding context reference and is most used in situations where a ViewModel hierarchy is present. In Knockout.JS, it is not so uncommon to host a child ViewModel inside a parent one. The `with` binding allows you to start using a child ViewModel from a child DOM node (more information on binding contexts is covered later in this chapter).

HTML templating

We introduced the `foreach` binding and now it's time to talk about HTML templating because the two concepts are tightly related each other.

HTML templating means that we can use a convenient approach to express complex DOM structures repeating or nesting a single HTML fragment that works as a reference template.

We can achieve a templating strategy in two ways:

- Built-in Knockout.JS templating
- Third-party JavaScript frameworks templating

Built-in Knockout.JS templating is based on the `foreach`, `if`/`ifnot`, and `with` bindings. The data-binding engine works using the contained DOM element as a reference template. For example, in a classic `foreach` binding, we have the following situation:

```
<div data-bind="foreach: items, visible: items().length > 0">
  <span data-bind="text: id"></span>
```

```
</div>
...
var ViewModel = function () {
  this.items = ko.observableArray([
    {
      id: 1
    }, {
      id: 2
    }
  ]);
};
ko.applyBindings(new ViewModel());
```

In the preceding example, Knockout.JS repeats the span tag inside the div element two times; the number of elements inside the items observable array. The span tag is the reference template because it's the HTML fragment contained inside the DOM element that declares the binding.

The runtime source result is the following:

```
<div data-bind="foreach: items, visible: items().length > 0">
    <span data-bind="text: id">1</span>
    <span data-bind="text: id">2</span>
</div>
```

There is no limit on how complex the HTML fragment template can be (in the previous example, everything placed inside the div tag would have been repeated two times).

It's possible to define the reference template outside the DOM element container. This means introducing a new special binding: the template binding. We can translate the previous example in the following way:

```
<div data-bind="template: { name: 'items-template', data: items },
visible: items().length > 0"></div>
<script type="text/html" id="items-template">
    <span data-bind="text: id"></span>
</script>
...
var ViewModel = function () {
  this.items = ko.observableArray([
    {
      id: 1
    }, {
```

```
        id: 2
    }
  ]);
};
ko.applyBindings(new ViewModel());
```

In the preceding example, the template bindings takes a literal object with two properties: the template ID (a template is defined with a script tag of the type text/html) and the ViewModel property (typically an array) that stores the data.

The final result is the same:

```
<div data-bind="template: { name: 'items-template', data: items },
visible: items().length > 0">
  <span data-bind="text: id">1</span>
  <span data-bind="text: id">2</span>
</div>
```

Knockout.JS also provides integration with other templating libraries such as **Underscore.JS**. They need a little bit of initial configuration (http://knockoutjs.com/documentation/template-binding.html).

The binding context

Having introduced the foreach, if/ifnot, and with bindings, it's also time to talk about the **binding context**, one of the most important, under the hood, Knockout.JS features.

Binding context is a sort of helper object created by the ko.applyBindings method. It's a dictionary of objects related to the View and the ViewModel and there are situations in which these objects are very useful to declare the data-bind attributes.

As I said, there are scenarios that make good use of nested ViewModel hierarchies, for example, when we have to realize complex UIs (think about something like Gmail), but also simpler cases in which an observable array contains elements that, in turn, hold observable properties (an element could be considered as a minimal ViewModel that exposes only data). These are the situations in which the binding context is very helpful for data-binding.

Accessing the binding context is very easy because Knockout.JS exposes a list of its properties that we can use in our `data-bind` attributes:

- `$data`: This is the current ViewModel, the one that the `data-bind` attributes refer to

- `$parent`: This is the parent ViewModel of the current one

- `$parents`: This is the ViewModel hierarchy of the current one (`$parents[0]` is the father, `$parents[1]` the grandfather, and so on)

- `$root`: This is the ViewModel hierarchy root

- `$index`: This is only available with the `foreach` data-binding, it's the zero-based index of the current array element

- `$context`: This is the current binding context (not used often)

- `$parentContext`: This is the parent of the current binding context (not used often)

- `$element`: This is the current DOM element, that is, the element that declares the current `data-bind` attribute

The simplest example we can think of to explain the binding context is the following:

```
<!DOCTYPE html>
<html>
<head lang="en">
    <meta charset="UTF-8">
    <title>Hello Knockout.JS</title>
</head>
<body>
    <table border="1" cellpadding="2">
        <thead>
        <tr>
            <th></th>
            <th>Book</th>
            <th></th>
        </tr>
        </thead>
        <tbody data-bind="foreach: books">
        <tr>
```

```
            <td data-bind="text: $index() + 1"></td>
            <td data-bind="text: $data"></td>
            <td>
                <input type="button" data-bind="click: $parent.
addToCart" value="Add to Cart" />
            </td>
        </tr>
        </tbody>
    </table>
    <script type="text/javascript" src="http://cdnjs.cloudflare.com/
ajax/libs/knockout/3.1.0/knockout-min.js"></script>
    <script type="text/javascript">
        var ViewModel = function () {
            this.books = ko.observable([
                "Patterns of Enterprise Application Architecture",
                "Domain-Driven Design: Tackling Complexity in the
Heart of Software",
                "Microsoft .net: Architecting Applications for the
Enterprise"]);
            this.addToCart = function (data) {
                alert(data + " added to Cart");
            };
        };
        ko.applyBindings(new ViewModel());
    </script>
</body>
</html>
```

In the preceding example, we used the `$data` identifier because it represents the current element of the array (during the `foreach` loop). This is the only way to access its value. It's not an object with properties that we can use to declare a binding in the HTML template (the `span` tags), but a simple string. Another thing to notice is the method invocation expression when using a binding context property in an inline function (in this case, `$index()`).

Here's the final result at runtime:

```
<tbody data-bind="foreach: books">
  <tr>
    <td data-bind="text: $index() + 1">1</td>
    <td data-bind="text: $data">Patterns of Enterprise Application
Architecture</td>
    <td>
      <input type="button" data-bind="click: $parent.addToCart"
value="Add to Cart">
    </td>
  </tr>
  <tr>
```

```
    <td data-bind="text: $index() + 1">2</td>
    <td data-bind="text: $data">Domain-Driven Design: Tackling
Complexity in the Heart of Software</td>
    <td>
      <input type="button" data-bind="click: $parent.addToCart"
value="Add to Cart">
    </td>
  </tr>
  <tr>
    <td data-bind="text: $index() + 1">3</td>
    <td data-bind="text: $data">Microsoft .net: Architecting
Applications for the Enterprise</td>
    <td>
      <input type="button" data-bind="click: $parent.addToCart"
value="Add to Cart">
    </td>
  </tr>
</tbody>
```

The following is the browser output:

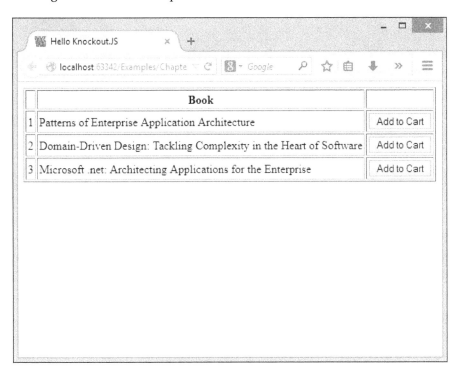

Another important aspect of this example is the `input` tag binding. We used the `$parent` property of the binding context to reference the ViewModel. The reason is that inside the `foreach` binding, the current binding context is referred to the current array element. This is why we need to traverse up to the parent (the ViewModel) to reach the `addToCart` method. If we analyze the `addToCart` definition, we will notice the `data` argument passed to the function. In a data-binding associated to a ViewModel method, the `$data` property of the binding context is automatically passed to the method. In fact, when we click on a button, the browser shows an alert with the related element value, for example, the second one:

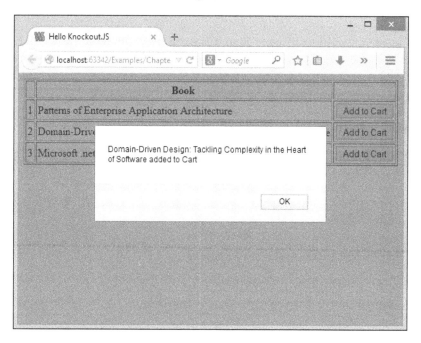

Virtual bindings

When there isn't a parent/child relationship between the DOM elements, it is not possible to apply a conditional or loop binding, but it is possible to use something equivalent. Virtual binding is the answer.

A virtual binding is a way to define a virtual DOM element with a conditional or loop binding using a particular syntax based on an HTML comment. The following is a simple example that shows how to define a virtual binding:

```
<!DOCTYPE html>
<html>
<head lang="en">
```

```
    <meta charset="UTF-8">
    <title>Hello Knockout.JS</title>
</head>
<body>
    <!-- ko foreach: items -->
        <p>
             + 
            <span data-bind="text: $index() + 1"></span>
             - 
            <span data-bind="text: $data"></span>
        </p>
    <!-- /ko -->
    <script type="text/javascript" src="//cdnjs.cloudflare.com/ajax/
libs/knockout/3.1.0/knockout-min.js"></script>
        var ViewModel = function () {
            this.items = ko.observable(["First", "Second", "Third"]);
        };
        ko.applyBindings(new ViewModel());
    </script>
</body>
</html>
```

In this example, the HTML comment notation, `<!-- ko --><!-- /ko -->`,
defines the virtual DOM element in which it is possible to declare a conditional
or loop binding.

At runtime, the HTML source is as follows:

```
<!-- ko foreach: items -->
<p>
 + 
<span data-bind="text: $index() + 1">1</span>
 - 
<span data-bind="text: $data">First</span>
</p>
<p>
 + 
<span data-bind="text: $index() + 1">2</span>
 - 
<span data-bind="text: $data">Second</span>
</p>
<p>
 + 
<span data-bind="text: $index() + 1">3</span>
 - 
<span data-bind="text: $data">Third</span>
</p>
<--! /ko -->
```

The following is the browser output:

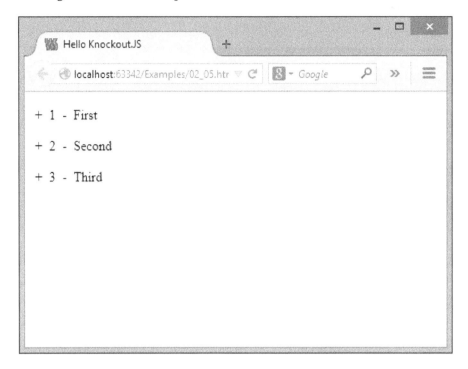

Form controls bindings

Knockout.JS provides a set of bindings that are specifically designed for form elements (input, select, button, and so on). Many of these are bindings that need an association to a ViewModel method (a command). Others are general purpose bindings, that is, they can be used in all DOM elements.

Form controls bindings are:

- click: This associates a ViewModel method (or inline function) to the DOM element click event. The $data property of the binding context and the JavaScript event object are automatically passed as arguments.

- event: This associates a ViewModel method (or inline function) to one or more DOM element events. The binding context $data property and the JavaScript event object are automatically passed as arguments.

- submit: This associates the form element's submit event to a ViewModel method (or an inline function). It's valid only for a form tag; don't use a click binding to manage a form submission.

- enable: This controls the activation state of a DOM element using a Boolean value.

- disable: This is the inverse version of the enable binding.

- value: This associates the value attribute of a DOM element (in particular, an input element) to a ViewModel property. This is particularly useful when we need to update an observable property from an input tag (a textbox for example). This binding allows an option named valueUpdate, which specifies when the update event is triggered (the default behavior is when the DOM element loses focus). There are three possible values:
    - input: This is triggered at every element value modification, keeping in sync the input tag content and the observable property (works only in modern browsers)
    - keyup: This is triggered at every keyup event
    - keypress: This is triggered at every keypress event; multiple events are triggered if a key is kept pressed
    - afterkeydown: This is triggered at every keypress event; no events are triggered if a key is kept pressed (similar to input and works in all browsers).

- hasfocus: This controls the focus state of a DOM element using a Boolean value.

- checked: This controls the checked state of an input element of the type checkbox or radio using a Boolean value.

- options: This associates the option tag's list of a select tag to an array of elements (usually a ViewModel observable array property). It's possible to use a simple array of strings, but also an array of complex objects. This binding allows a series of other options. The most important are:
    - optionsText: This is the array element property name that specifies the text attribute of the option tag (needed when the array elements are complex)
    - optionsValue: This is the array element property name that specifies the value attribute of the option tag (needed when the array elements are complex)
    - optionsCaption: This is the text of a typical "Select an item please." option tag (this element is not needed to be present in the ViewModel array)

- ○ value: This associates the selected array element (that corresponds with the selected option tag) to a ViewModel property when the select tag allows only a single selection

- ○ selectedOptions: This associates the selected array elements (that correspond with the selected option tag) to a ViewModel observable array property when the select tag allows multiple selections

- uniqueName: This ensures that the DOM element has a nonempty, unique name attribute if not already present. It's possible to declare this binding only in the following form: uniqueName: true.

Custom bindings

One of the most important Knockout.JS features is extensibility. This is particularly true for bindings. Even though Knockout.JS provides a wide variety of data-bind options, it's possible to define custom bindings.

The objective of a custom binding is to wrap a particular behavior in a form that can be used in Knockout.JS in a way that is compliant with the Model-View-ViewModel pattern.

It is worth looking at the following examples to depict how a custom binding works. The first example shows how we can utilize a numeric slider using a classic jQuery UI approach:

```
<!DOCTYPE html>
<html>
<head lang="en">
    <meta charset="UTF-8">
    <title>jQuery UI Slider</title>
    <link rel="stylesheet" href="//ajax.googleapis.com/ajax/libs/
jqueryui/1.10.4/themes/smoothness/jquery-ui.css" />
</head>
<body>
    <p>
        <span>Slider value:</span>
         
        <span id="sliderValue"></span>
         
```

```
            <button id="sliderReset">Reset</button>
    </p>
    <div id="slider"></div>
        <script type="text/JavaScript" src="//ajax.googleapis.com/ajax/
    libs/jquery/1.11.0/jquery.min.js"></script>
        <script type="text/JavaScript" src="//ajax.googleapis.com/ajax/
    libs/jqueryui/1.10.4/jquery-ui.min.js"></script>
        <script type="text/JavaScript">
            jQuery("#slider").slider({
                value: 100,
                min: 0,
                max: 500,
                step: 50,
                slide: function(event, ui) {
                    jQuery("#sliderValue")
                        .text(ui.value );
                }
            });
            jQuery("#sliderValue")
                .text(jQuery("#slider")
                .slider("value"));
            jQuery("#sliderReset").on("click", function() {
                jQuery("#slider").slider({
                    value: 100
                });
                jQuery("#sliderValue")
                    .text(jQuery("#slider")
                    .slider("value"));
            });
        </script>
    </body>
    </html>
```

This is pretty straightforward. We used JQuery and JQuery UI to add a numeric slider to the page using a `div` tag. There is also a `span` tag used to show the slider value and a `button` tag that resets the slider to the initial value. The JavaScript code is quite simple. First, there is the slider initialization, then the `span` tag receives the initial slider value, and finally, the button `click` event handler that resets the slider initial value. In the slider initialization, we also defined the `slide` event handler in which the `tag` span text is updated every time the user moves the handle. As already mentioned, this is a classic jQuery approach. Everything is managed using a direct reference to the tag IDs and the well-known fluent interface programming style.

The following is the final result:

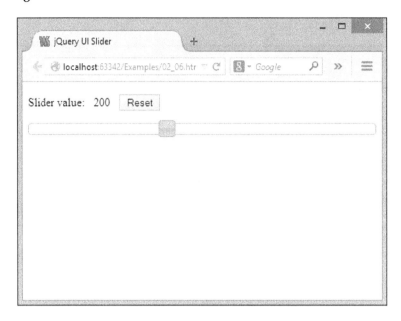

We can achieve the same result using a custom binding:

```html
<!DOCTYPE html>
<html>
<head lang="en">
    <meta charset="UTF-8">
    <title>Custom Binding - Knockout.JS</title>
    <link rel="stylesheet" href="//ajax.googleapis.com/ajax/libs/
jqueryui/1.10.4/themes/smoothness/jquery-ui.css" />
</head>
<body>
    <p>
        <span>Slider value:</span>
         
        <span data-bind="text: amount"></span>
         
        <button data-bind="click: reset">Reset</button>
    </p>
    <div data-bind="slider: amount"></div>
    <script type="text/JavaScript" src="//ajax.googleapis.com/ajax/
libs/jquery/1.11.0/jquery.min.js"></script>
```

```
    <script type="text/JavaScript" src="//ajax.googleapis.com/ajax/
libs/jqueryui/1.10.4/jquery-ui.min.js"></script>
    <script type="text/javascript" src="//cdnjs.cloudflare.com/ajax/
libs/knockout/3.1.0/knockout-min.js"></script>
    <script type="text/JavaScript">
        ko.bindingHandlers.slider = {
            init: function(element, valueAccessor, allBindings,
viewModel, bindingContext) {
                var property = valueAccessor();
                jQuery(element).slider({
                    value: ko.unwrap(property),
                    min: 0,
                    max: 500,
                    step: 50,
                    slide: function(event, ui) {
                        property(ui.value);
                    }
                });
            },
            update: function(element, valueAccessor, allBindings,
viewModel, bindingContext) {
                var property = valueAccessor();
                jQuery(element).slider({
                    value: ko.unwrap(property)
                });
            }
        };
        var ViewModel = function () {
            var self = this;
            self.amount = ko.observable(100);
            self.reset = function() {
                self.amount(100);
            };
        };
        ko.applyBindings(new ViewModel());
    </script>
</body>
</html>
```

The HTML markup is the same as the previous example with a single difference. We don't have the id attribute anymore, but the data-bind attribute. The first JavaScript instruction defines the new custom binding named slider (the one we used in the div tag). A custom binding is defined as a new property of the built-in ko.bindingHandlers object. This property, in turn, is a literal object that contains two functions:

- init: This is called just once at the ko.applyBindings invocation. It's the place in which we define the initial state of the DOM element and attach every event handler needed to update the associated observable object.

- update: This is called every time the associated observable object changes its state. It's the place in which we update the DOM element based on the new observable value.

Both the functions have the same argument list:

- element: This is the DOM element that declares the binding.

- valueAccessor: This is a JavaScript function used to access the underlying ViewModel property. To obtain the value of the property, it is a good practice to call the helper method, ko.unwrap, because it takes into account whether the property is observable or not.

- allBindings: This is a JavaScript function used to access all the other bindings declared in the current DOM element.

- viewModel: This argument is deprecated in the latest Knockout.JS versions. It's the current ViewModel.

- bindingContext: This is the current binding context (if you want to access the ViewModel in the latest Knockout.JS versions, use bindingContext.$data).

In this example, we initialized the slider using the element argument in the init function. We also got a reference to the ViewModel property calling valueAccessor, using its value to initialize the first slider state (calling ko.unwrap) and setting the new value inside the slide event handler. In the update function, we set the slider state using the ViewModel property value.

The ViewModel is very simple. We defined the amount numeric property and a reset command that simply set the amount property to its initial value. What's interesting here is that we can use the same ViewModel property to manage both the span tag that shows the slider value and the div tag that becomes the slider itself.

Once ko.applyBindings is called, the custom binding enters the init functions, creates the slider using jQuery UI, and registers the slide event handler in which it will change the ViewModel property value. When the button is clicked, the reset method is invoked and the amount property is changed. The custom binding calls the update function in which the slider value is modified accordingly.

The following is the final result, identical to the first one:

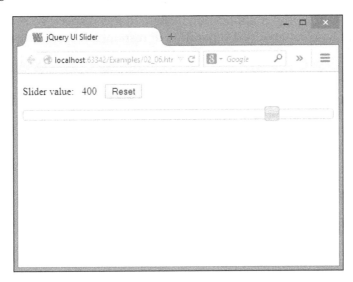

The difference between the two examples is quite evident. Using Knockout.JS with a custom binding, we achieved a real separation between the presentation logic and user interface. The ViewModel is clearly an abstraction in which we can express what happens in our application conceptually. In this example, we know that if a reset command is invoked, the amount is brought back to 100. This is the business logic. It doesn't matter how we physically represent these concepts on the web page. On the other hand, the user interface, the View, is clean. We didn't use any tag id attribute and that is good because in a complex HTML page, with many tags, it's not always easy to assure an identifier's uniqueness. All the code that connects the user interface and ViewModel is placed in a proper reusable structure: a custom binding.

A custom binding has two main characteristics. It's a reusable piece of code so we can build our personal custom bindings library, and it's the right tool to embed a complex UI behavior in a way compliant with the Model-View-ViewModel pattern.

There is a lot more to say about custom binding. I suggest you dig into this topic on the Knockout.JS website (http://knockoutjs.com/documentation/custom-bindings.html).

Summary

This chapter is a starting point to learn about how Knockout.JS works. It gives the overall understanding of the Model-View-ViewModel presentation pattern and the most important technical details of this library.

If you look at the big picture, it's easier to see how these techniques foster better web application testing. It's virtually impossible to adequately test a web application without a proper application design. In this respect, you have learned how Knockout.JS promotes a real separation of responsibilities between the View and ViewModel.

In the next chapter, we will dig into a well-known JavaScript unit testing framework. Then, we will put all together to understand how we can take advantage of Knockout.JS in a web application testing strategy.

3
The Jasmine Unit Testing Framework Explained

Web application testing is a complex topic because there are several types of testing from unit testing to integration testing, through several other categorizations that can be involved in a complete test strategy.

The question is where do we start? I think the best answer to this question is from the house foundations, where anything strong and solid should start. The main objective of this book is to explain web application testing using a JavaScript library that implements a well-known presentation design pattern (**Model-View-ViewModel**). In this scenario, the core of a testing strategy is definitely **unit testing**.

In this chapter, we will introduce **Jasmine**, a unit testing JavaScript library that uses a **Behavior Driven Development** (**BDD**) style to examine the various units and modules of the source code. In particular, we will use Version 2.0.

You will learn:

- What is BDD and how we can think about testing this way
- How Jasmine works and what kind of tools it provides

Unit testing style

There are plenty of books that talk about software testing in terms of design principles and development processes (for example, **Test Driven Development**). This book, on the other hand, is a sort of hands-on manual that tries to explain the fundamental patterns, technologies, and tools involved in web application testing. This means that the main objective here is not to discuss the big picture of software testing; however, every unit testing framework is inspired by a specific style, so we need to briefly talk about it.

One of the most known techniques about testing is TDD or Test Driven Development, but it is a mistake to think that TDD is simply related to unit testing. TDD is a software development process that pursues a good code design using unit testing as a means to reach its objective.

According to Kent Beck's book *Test-Driven Development by Example*, TDD is a technique expressed through the repetition of the following steps: add a test, run all the tests and see if the new one fails, write some code necessary to pass the tests, run the tests, and refactor the code.

This process aims to produce better code by writing the tests first. Developers are forced to think about testability from the very beginning. This also leads to a better understanding of the functional and nonfunctional requirements.

TDD is not the only technique based on some sort of code testing. BDD is also related to unit testing and TDD itself. BDD has recently been developed by **Dan North**. Its objective is to revise the approach of unit testing bearing in mind the final user acceptance criteria.

TDD doesn't mention at all where to start, how much code needs to be tested, and what's more important in a complex codebase. BDD tries to answer these questions. It provides guidelines to help developers feel comfortable with unit testing. For example, BDD suggests a specific way to name tests and suites; one of the most surprising issues in TDD. Also, BDD enforces a new mindset; not simply tests, but behaviors. In this way, we can improve our overall system understanding because we need to focus on its final behavior, not a single technical test.

BDD starts from the **user stories** as means to express system requirements, and defines a particular form to express tests. The format of the form is the following:

```
Given [initial context]
When [event occurs]
Then [ensure some outcomes]
```

This approach is a good example of how developers can close the gap between technical details of software development and system analysis, or the user acceptance criteria.

Jasmine has been designed this way. Its API follows this schema and helps developers to focus on the code behavior in terms of execution contexts, events (usually triggered by the user), and expected outcomes.

Hello Jasmine

Working with Jasmine is quite easy. We have to perform the following steps:

1. Download Jasmine 2.0 as a ZIP file from its hosting website on **Github** (`https://github.com/pivotal/jasmine/tree/master/dist`).

2. Create a folder for the test project.

3. Unzip the Jasmine package inside the folder created in step 2.

4. Empty the `spec` and `src` subfolders deleting the example files.

5. Add some source code to be tested in the `src` subfolder as `.js` files.

6. Add some testing code using Jasmine in the `spec` subfolder as `.js` files.

7. Add script references to the files added in steps 5 and 6 to the special file, `SpecRunner.html`.

8. Open `SpecRunner.html` in a web browser to run the tests and verify the results.

This is clearly not a typical TDD coding cycle. We first write some code and then we test it. TDD suggests the exact opposite. I'm a great TDD supporter, but I want to keep things here as simple as possible and explain Jasmine even to those who do not know TDD.

For example, in step 5, we can add the following JavaScript file, named `03_01.js`, with a simple source code to be tested:

```
var MyClass = function () {
    this.message = "Hello Jasmine!";
};
```

This class is simple, but here the objective is to learn how to set up a Jasmine project.

In step 6, we can add the following JavaScript file, named `03_01_spec.js`, with some testing code:

```
describe("Given MyClass implementation", function () {
    var myObj = new MyClass();
    it("when accessing message, then it should be equal to \"Hello
Jasmine!\"", function () {
        expect(myObj.message).toEqual("Hello Jasmine!");
    });
});
```

I will explain how Jasmine works, in detail, in the next sections, but this first simple example shows very well that we can express our tests in the BDD style using the **given\when\then** form.

In the Jasmine's `describe` global function (called `suite`), we pass a given sentence that defines the context (an object that implements `MyClass`), and a function that will be executed by the spec runner. In this function, we initialize the `myObj` object of type `MyClass` and then we call the Jasmine method, `it`.

In the `it` global function (called `specification`), we pass a when/then sentence specifying a circumstance (accessing the `message` property) and verification (the `message` property has to be equal to `"Hello Jasmine!"`). Then, a function that will be executed by the spec runner in which we express our expectations using the Jasmine global function, `expect`.

In step 7, we have to add the following file references to `SpecRunner_03_01.html`:

```
<!DOCTYPE HTML>
<html>
<head>
    <meta http-equiv="Content-Type" content="text/html;
charset=UTF-8">
    <title>Jasmine Spec Runner v2.0.0</title>
    <link rel="shortcut icon" type="image/png" href="libs/
jasmine-2.0.0/jasmine_favicon.png">
    <link rel="stylesheet" type="text/css" href="libs/jasmine-2.0.0/
jasmine.css">
    <script type="text/javascript" src="libs/jasmine-2.0.0/jasmine.
js"></script>
    <script type="text/javascript" src="libs/jasmine-2.0.0/jasmine-
html.js"></script>
    <script type="text/javascript" src="libs/jasmine-2.0.0/boot.js"></
script>
    <!-- include source files here... -->
    <script type="text/javascript" src="src/03_01.js"></script>
    <!-- include spec files here... -->
    <script type="text/javascript" src="specs/03_01_specs.js"></
script>
</head>
<body>
</body>
</html>
```

Running this page in a web browser, we obtain the following result:

The `SpecRunner_03_01.html` file is a very simple page. There is a summary bar that shows how many specifications have been executed and how many have failed. Then, for every suite, it shows the **given** sentence and all the specific **when/then** sentences.

In this first example, the unique specification that we wrote passes successfully: everything in the spec runner page is green, the summary bar and the expectation sentence.

We can try to simulate a test failure with the following `03_02_specs.js` specifications file:

```
describe("Given MyClass implementation", function () {
    var myObj = new MyClass();
    it("when accessing message, then it should not be null", function
() {
        expect(myObj.message).not.toBeNull();
    });
    it("when accessing message, then it should be equal to \"Hello
Jasmine!\"", function () {
        expect(myObj.message).toEqual("This is not the right
message!");
    });
});
```

There are two specifications; the second one is clearly false. When we execute a second spec runner, SpecRunner_03_02.html that points to this file, we get the following result:

The summary bar is red because there is at least one specification failure. The page shows all the failures' details immediately, but we can switch to the specifications list by clicking on the **Spec List** menu item:

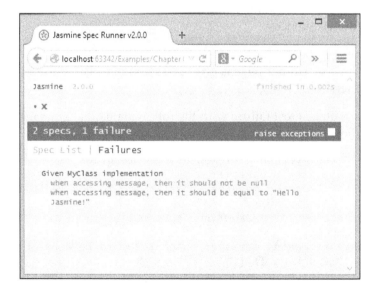

The specifications list shows all the successes in green and all those that have failed in red.

Suites and specifications

In the previous example, we saw that Jasmine is quite simple to use, even if we decided not to express our tests in a real BDD style. Its working pattern is always defined by a sequence of suites that contains a sequence of specifications, which, in turn, contains one or more expectations.

Suites

The `describe` Jasmine global function defines a suite that we can describe as a container for a given broad context (or more generally, if we don't want to think in BDD, a logical specifications grouping):

```
describe("a suite or context for specifications", function () {
  //a sequence of specifications
});
```

The `describe` function accepts two arguments: a string representing a sentence that expresses the suite/context and a function that contains all the code needed to execute the suite itself, mostly specifications.

It's also possible to nest in the suites calling one or more `describe` functions inside a parent `describe` function. This is useful when you have to narrow a big context in a smaller one and maintain the final spec runner result readable:

```
//big context
describe("users can create a profile", function () {
    //smaller context
    describe("email address is correct format", function () {
    //expectations
    });
});
```

We can disable a suite execution using the alternative function, `xdescribe`; this suite will not run during the spec runner execution. This is useful when you want to focus on a specific aspect of the software and don't want to execute all the suites. You simply put an x before the `describe` method call.

Specifications

The `it` Jasmine global function defines a specification that we can define as a precise circumstance of the general context, which we have to verify (in BDD, we need to identify the **when** event and the **then** assumption):

```
describe("a suite or context for specifications", function () {
  it("a precise circumstance of the context", function () {
    //a sequence of expectations
  });
});
```

This function is similar to `describe` because it accepts two arguments: a string representing a sentence that expresses the given circumstance and a function that contains all the code needed to execute the specification, mostly expectations.

We can disable a specification execution using the alternative function, `xit`, simply placing `x` before the `it` method call (for the same reason as the `xdescribe` method). This specification will not run during the spec runner execution, and will be shown as suspended in the spec runner UI. A specification will be shown as pending if it also calls the `pending` global function anywhere in the specification body.

Setup and teardown

It's important to understand that the `describe` and `it` global functions will not only contain specifications and expectations respectively. It's always necessary to add some more code to set up the complete and working tests, for example, code needed to implement all the objects involved in what we are verifying and all the method calls that trigger the specifications events that we need to stress on.

There are two Jasmine global functions that help setting up a proper test execution environment: `beforeEach` and `afterEach`. Like every other unit testing framework, Jasmine provides these two functions to set up and teardown a specification context. In the `beforeEach` function, we have to write all the code needed to create and initialize all the objects that we need to execute a single specification. The `afterEach` function is used to reset all these objects. They both take a function as a single argument, which will be executed by the spec runner.

Jasmine calls these two functions once for every `it` specification, before and after their execution (as their name suggests). In this way, we can reset and initialize a clean context, so that we can run each specification independently from the others:

```
describe("a suite or context for specifications", function () {
  var aVariable, anotherVariable;
```

```
beforeEach(function () {
  //setup test environment
  aVariable = {…};
  anotherVariable = {…};
});
afterEach(function () {
  //reset test environment
  aVariable = null;
  anotherVariable = null;
});
it("a first precise circumstance of the context", function () {
  //a sequence of expectations
  });
it("a second precise circumstance of the context", function () {
  //a sequence of expectations
  });
});
```

Expectations and matchers

The core of a specification is expectations; the part of the code that literally executes the tests, trying to verify if the assumptions are met.

Jasmine provides a global function called `expect`, and a series of functions called matchers to build and verify an expectation. In the first example of this chapter, we used the following expectation:

```
describe("Given MyClass implementation", function () {
    var myObj = new MyClass();
    it("when accessing message, then it should be equal to \"Hello
Jasmine!\"", function () {
        expect(myObj.message).toEqual("Hello Jasmine!");
    });
});
```

The `expect` function takes the target variable as the argument. We can then chain a matcher function (in this case, `toEqual`) that takes the value we want to compare with the target variable as the argument. Every matcher function returns the Boolean value `true` if the comparison is met and `false` if the comparison is not met.

We can also negate a matcher by placing the `not` property just before the matcher itself:

```
describe("Given MyClass implementation", function () {
    var myObj = new MyClass();
    it("when accessing message, then it should be equal to \"Hello
Jasmine!\"", function () {
        expect(myObj.message).not.toEqual("Hello Jasmine!");
    });
});
```

For the spec runner, a specification fails if there are one or more false expectations and is successful if all the expectations are true.

Jasmine provides an exhaustive list of built-in matchers:

- `toBe`: This executes a `===` comparison
- `toEqual`: This executes an equality applicable to simple data type (numeric, string, and so on)
- `toMatch`: This executes a regular expression comparison
- `toBeDefined`, `toBeUndefined`: This executes a comparison with `undefined`
- `toBeNull`: This executes a comparison with `null`
- `toBeTruthy`, `toBeFalsy`: This executes a comparison using a Boolean casting
- `toContain`: This verifies if an item is present in an array
- `toBeLessThan`, `toBeGreaterThan`: This executes a numerical comparison
- `toBeCloseTo`: This executes a precision mathematical comparison
- `toThrow`: This verifies whether a function throws an exception (the `expect` function takes another function as an argument)

Usually, these matchers are enough to cover all the needs. However, it is possible to define custom matchers using a dedicated Jasmine API (more information can be found on the Jasmine website, `http://jasmine.github.io/`).

In JavaScript, there are two different equality operators: == and ===. It's very important to understand their behavior so as to not make mistakes in expectations.

The == operator is called the normal equality. It checks two values, converts them to a common type, and returns true if both are equal. The === operator is called the strict equality. It doesn't make the implicit conversion; it compares values and also the types. Douglas Crockford, in his book *JavaScript: The Good Parts*, writes: *"JavaScript has two sets of equality operators: === and !==, and their evil twins == and !=. The good ones work the way you would expect. If the two operands are of the same type and have the same value, then === produces true and !== produces false. The evil twins do the right thing when the operands are of the same type, but if they are of different types, they attempt to coerce the values. the rules by which they do that are complicated and unmemorable."*

Usually, code quality tools such as JSLint mark the normal equality operator, ==, as an error to avoid.

Spies

A test double is a fundamental topic, which talks about unit testing. Jasmine provides its own implementation called **spies**.

A test double is a particular object used to replace another object originally involved in the code under the test. Usually, a test double is a simplified version of the original one that behaves the same way and can be easily controlled during the test execution. The objective is to isolate the test execution context from everything that is not directly related to the test subject. In other words, if we want to test the behavior of a particular object that has some sort of interaction with other objects, we need something to tightly control the latter so that we can accurately define the execution context.

A spy is a function that can stub any other function and track all the calls and every argument passed. The following example (03_03_specs.js) shows the basic spy functionality. Remember that here we want to show how it works technically, not how we can take advantage of a test double in a real-world scenario (this is a topic that we will cover in the next chapter):

```
describe("Given a generic function", function () {
    var container = {
```

```
    myFunc: function (aNumber) {
        return aNumber + 1;
    }
};
it("when using a spy, then it tracks all the calls", function () {
    //create a spy on myFun
    spyOn(container, "myFunc");
    //call myFunc twice
    container.myFunc(10);
    container.myFunc(20);
    //verify calls to myFunc
    expect(container.myFunc).toHaveBeenCalled();
    expect(container.myFunc).toHaveBeenCalledWith(10);
    expect(container.myFunc).toHaveBeenCalledWith(20);
});
});
```

The result is a green spec runner (SpecRunner_03_03.html):

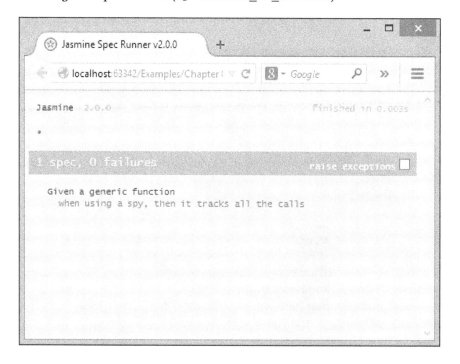

Creating a spy is very simple. We used the `spyOn` Jasmine global function passing the object that contains the method we want to track, and the name of that method as arguments. Then, we made some calls to that method (now transformed into a spy) and we verified some expectations using the dedicated spy matchers, `toHaveBeenCalled` and `toHaveBeenCalledWith`.

These matcher names speak for themselves; the first one verifies whether the method has been called at least once, the second one verifies whether the method has been called by passing some specific arguments (one argument in this example). Notice that we called the `myFunc` method twice and the spy tracked all of the calls with all the arguments that we passed.

A spy created in this way is called a stub. A call to the `myFunc` method doesn't execute the original method because it has been replaced by the spy itself (a spy doesn't return anything, so the return value is `undefined`).

Spy initialization options

There are several options that we can use during a spy initialization:

- `callThrough`: The spy will redirect every call to the original method with this option:

  ```
  spyOn(container, "myFunc").and.callThrough();
  ```

- `returnValue`: The spy will always return a specific value that we specify with this option:

  ```
  spyOn(container, "myFunc").and.returnValue(50);
  ```

- `callFake`: The spy will redirect every call to the function that we specify with this option:

  ```
  spyOn(container, "myFunc").and.callFake(function (arg) {
    return arg + 10;
  });
  ```

- `throwError`: The spy will always throw the error that we specify with this option:

  ```
  spyOn(container, "myFunc").and.throwError("this is an exception");
  ```

- `stub`: The spy will become a simple stub again, no matter how it was initialized before with this option:

  ```
  container.myFunc.and.stub();
  ```

The following example summarizes all these initialization options
(`03_04_specs.js`):

```javascript
describe("Given a generic function", function () {
    var container;
    beforeEach(function () {
        container = {
            myFunc: function (aNumber) {
                return aNumber + 1;
            }
        };
    });
    afterEach(function () {
        container = null;
    });
    it("when using a spy callTrough, then it redirects all the calls
to the original method", function () {
        var result;
        spyOn(container, "myFunc").and.callThrough();
        result = container.myFunc(10);
        expect(container.myFunc).toHaveBeenCalled();
        expect(container.myFunc).toHaveBeenCalledWith(10);
        expect(result).toEqual(11);
    });
    it("when using a spy returnValue, then it returns the value
specified", function () {
        var result;
        spyOn(container, "myFunc").and.returnValue(50);
        result = container.myFunc(10);
        expect(container.myFunc).toHaveBeenCalled();
        expect(container.myFunc).toHaveBeenCalledWith(10);
        expect(result).toEqual(50);
    });
    it("when using a spy callFake, then it calls the function
specified", function () {
        var result;
        spyOn(container, "myFunc").and.callFake(function (arg) {
            return arg + 10;
        });
        result = container.myFunc(10);
        expect(container.myFunc).toHaveBeenCalled();
        expect(container.myFunc).toHaveBeenCalledWith(10);
        expect(result).toEqual(20);
    });
```

```
    it("when using a spy throwError, then it throws the exception
specified", function () {
        spyOn(container, "myFunc").and.throwError("this is an
exception");
        expect(function () {
            container.myFunc(10);
        }).toThrowError("this is an exception");
    });
    it("when using a spy stub, then it becomes a simple stub",
function () {
        var result;
        spyOn(container, "myFunc").and.callThrough();
        result = container.myFunc(10);
        expect(result).toEqual(11);
        container.myFunc.and.stub();
        result = container.myFunc(20);
        expect(container.myFunc).toHaveBeenCalled();
        expect(container.myFunc).toHaveBeenCalledWith(10);
        expect(container.myFunc).toHaveBeenCalledWith(20);
        expect(result).toBeUndefined();
    });
});
```

The result is a green spec runner (SpecRunner_03_04.html):

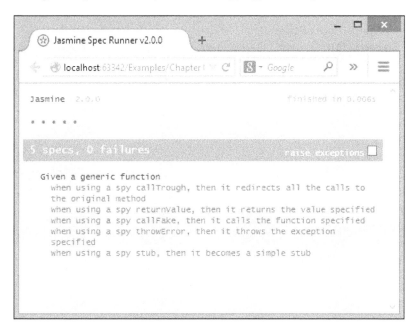

Spy tracking properties

The spy tracking functionality not only allows verifying whether a method has been called and what arguments were passed, but it also provides a series of additional statistics through the `calls` property (refer to the `SpecRunner_03_05.html` example):

- any: This verifies whether the spy has ever been called:

```
expect(container.myFunc.calls.any()).toEqual(true);
```

- count: This returns the total number of calls:

```
expect(container.myFunc.calls.count()).toEqual(2);
```

- argsFor: This returns a list of arguments of the nth call (array):

```
expect(container.myFunc.calls.argsFor(0)).toEqual([10]);
```

- allArgs: This returns a list of arguments of all the calls (array of arrays):

```
expect(container.myFunc.calls.allArgs()).toEqual([
    [10],
    [20]
]);
```

- all: This returns the `this` context object and a list of arguments of all the calls (array of objects):

```
expect(container.myFunc.calls.all()).toEqual([
  {
    object: container,
    args: [10]
  },
  {
    object: container,
    args: [20]
  }
]);
```

- mostRecent: This returns the `this` context object and a list of arguments of the last call:

```
expect(container.myFunc.calls.mostRecent()).toEqual({
  object: container,
  args: [20]
});
```

- `first`: This returns the `this` context object and a list of arguments of the first call:

```
expect(container.myFunc.calls.first()).toEqual({
  object: container,
  args: [10]
});
```

- `reset`: This clears all the tracked calls in the spy:

```
container.myFunc.calls.reset();
```

An alternative spy initialization API

The `spyOn` global function works for an existing object if we want to spy on one of its methods. Jasmine also provides two more functions that can create a spy, without the need of an existing object (refer to the `SpecRunner_03_06.html` example):

- `createSpy`: This creates a pure spy without any real method behind it:

```
//create a spy
var mySpy = jasmine.createSpy("mySpy");
//call the spy
mySpy(23, "an argument");
//verify expectations as a regular spy
expect(mySpy).toHaveBeenCalled();
expect(mySpy).toHaveBeenCalledWith(23, "an argument");
```

- `createSpyObj`: This creates a mock object with one or more pure spies at once:

```
//create a mock with spies
var myMock = jasmine.createSpyObj("myMock", ["aSpy",
"anotherSpy"]);
//call the spies
myMock.aSpy();
myMock.anotherSpy(10);
//verify expectations as regular spies
expect(myMock.aSpy).toHaveBeenCalled();
expect(myMock.aSpy.calls.argsFor(0).length).toEqual(0);
expect(myMock.anotherSpy).toHaveBeenCalled();
expect(myMock.anotherSpy).toHaveBeenCalledWith(10);
```

Testing asynchronous code

Jasmine can test asynchronous code using an alternative specification pattern. The beforeEach, afterEach, and it global functions can receive an argument, which is a particular helper function that we have to use in this situation.

The asynchronous test pattern can be summarized in the following example (03_07.js). Think about a typical service that executes an ajax request:

```
var MyService = function () {
    this.fetchResult = function (callback) {
        jQuery.ajax("url", {
            success: function (result) {
                callback(result);
            }
        });
    };
};
```

The fetchResult method takes a callback function as an argument, which is called by passing the result when the Ajax call is successful.

If we want to test this JavaScript class, we can write the following spec (03_07_specs.js):

```
describe("Given an async service", function () {
    var myService, myResult;
    beforeEach(function (done) {
        myService = new MyService();
        spyOn(myService, "fetchResult").and.callFake(function
(callback) {
            setTimeout(function () {
                callback(10);
                done();
            }, 50);
        });
        myService.fetchResult(function (result) {
            myResult = result;
        });
    });
    it("when service is tested with the async pattern, then it can be
simulated", function (done) {
        expect(myResult).toEqual(10);
        done();
    });
});
```

In the `beforeEach` global function, we initialized a `MyService` instance. Then, we created a spy on its `fetchResult` method, which fakes an asynchronous call using the JavaScript `setTimeout` function. The fake function takes the same argument as the original method, a callback. In this way, we can recreate the original scenario. We simply don't make a real Ajax call or fetch any real remote result, but we set that result explicitly. The final step consists of calling the spy to start the test.

In the specification `it` global function, we simply verify the expectation.

The most important thing to notice here is that we highlighted the `done` argument, that is, the helper function we mentioned earlier. When we specify this optional argument, both in the `beforeEach` and `it` functions, we are instructing Jasmine that we are testing some asynchronous code and it has to behave differently. In fact, in this suite, the `it` specification function is not called until the `done` function is called in the `beforeEach` body. Again, the spec is not considered complete until the same `done` function is not invoked in the `it` body.

The result is a green spec runner (`SpecRunner_03_07.html`):

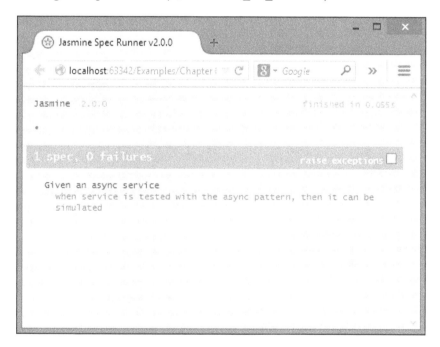

Summary

This chapter is a brief introduction to the Jasmine BBD test framework. It's not intended to be an exhaustive reference, but it gives a sufficient comprehension of how it works and how it can help a developer focus on the code behavior.

You learned about the fundamental Jasmine concepts. First of all, you learned how to set up a complete test project using the package downloaded from the project website. Then, we dug into the way the Jasmine API has been designed, and how to express our test in terms of suites, specifications, and expectations.

You also learned that we can create test doubles using spies, and we reviewed all the tracking capabilities that we can take advantage of.

Finally, we discovered how to test asynchronous code explaining how to solve the typical Ajax scenario.

In the next chapter, we will put the two main book topics together. We will try to explain how to test a Knockout.JS web application effectively using Jasmine, not only technically speaking, but also in the broader context of the application design.

4
Unit Testing Strategies

Testing a software solution is not only a question of technologies; actually, it's more a question of development strategies. For example, the most important objective of **Test Driven Development** (**TDD**) is a good overall design of a software solution. TDD is a specific development strategy and it's achieved through unit testing and its tools and frameworks.

It's very important to say that TDD and unit testing are not synonyms, and they're not related to the same concept even if they are complementary. TDD uses unit testing as a way to express a particular development style, but the latter can also be used in a development environment that is not based on TDD. In fact, we can simply write unit tests because we need to avoid regression errors, or because we want to focus on a single software module at a time and need to mock other dependent modules.

There is not enough space in this book to talk extensively about TDD because too many concepts are involved in this discipline, not only unit testing. Obviously, you can apply TDD or any other development process you prefer, but here we want to illustrate how to plan a web application solution with general unit testing in mind.

In this chapter, you will learn:

- Why it's a good idea to use a presentation design pattern when you need to test a web application
- How to structure a JavaScript web solution in terms of folders and files
- How to deal with **Model-View-ViewModel** (**MVVM**) in unit testing, using **Knockout.JS** and **Jasmine**
- How to manage services and third-party libraries
- How to write integration and use case unit test specifications

My Todo sample application

In this chapter, we will discuss all the fundamental concepts using a sample solution: a simple to-do list website called **My Todo**. In this way, we can dig into the various development aspects that are important when we talk about testing.

This is an elementary **Single Page Application (SPA)** that we can create a mock-up of as shown in the following screenshot:

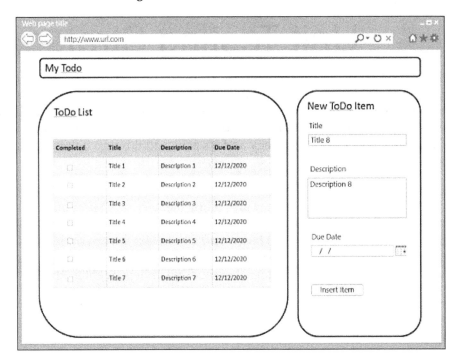

The main page shows two sections: the to-do item list on the left and the new to-do item form on the right. Everyone can imagine the basic functionality:

- The to-do item list shows all the current to-do items, generally loaded from a remote service
- The new to-do item form is the place to add all the information for a new item

Everything is simple and straightforward, but it's a good base to start and understand how to set up and properly manage a JavaScript solution.

The solution structure

A good solution structure is very important to organize the code base and development process correctly. In this chapter, I will use **Jetbrains Webstorm**, one of the most known JavaScript IDE (`http://www.jetbrains.com/webstorm/`).

Generally speaking, the solution structure depends directly upon the adopted technology; usually, a web application is not a pure JavaScript client solution, but it's built in a specific server technology environment, such as PHP, Ruby, ASP.NET, and JSP.

However, we can define a typical folder organization that is always valid for the JavaScript codebase because it lives quite independently from the server-side counterpart.

We can set up the following folders:

- The project's root folder: This is the main project folder. It contains all the HTML page files.
- `styles`: This folder contains all the CSS files, fonts, and similar resources (LESS, SASS, and so on).
- `scripts`: This folder contains all the JavaScript code and tests' files:
  - `libs`: This folder contains all the JavaScript third-party libraries and frameworks (for example jQuery, Knockout.JS, and so on).
  - `src`: This contains all the solution source code JavaScript files.
  - `tests`: This is the Jasmine project folder. It contains the same files and subfolders we saw in *Chapter 3*, *The Jasmine Unit Testing Framework Explained*, plus all the specification JavaScript files.

In the following screenshot, we can spot the previous folder organizations applied to the My Todo solution:

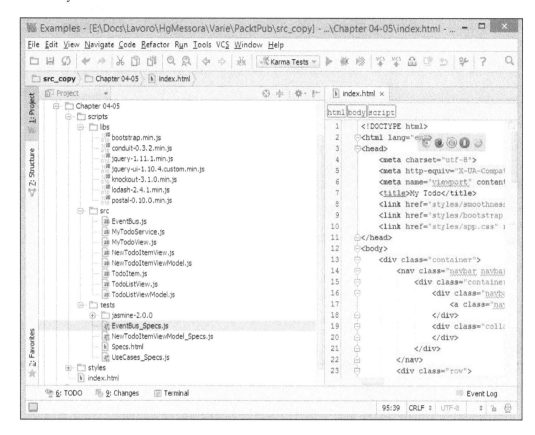

Also, this is a good starting point for other tools and processes that we can use to develop our solution, such as test automation, code quality inspectors, and code minification (we will introduce these technologies in the next chapter).

Idiomatic JavaScript patterns

Every programming language has its own idiomatic patterns. They are design patterns that can be expressed using the specific characteristics and syntax of that programming language.

Our objective is to write good code, which can be tested in the simplest possible way. If we learn how to effectively use JavaScript, we can write clean code and avoid a certain number of additional tests.

There are two idiomatic patterns that are very important in our scenario. We will extensively use them throughout all the My Todo solution:

- Constructor functions
- Module pattern

Obviously, there are many other patterns and techniques that are extremely useful, for example, **Asynchronous Module Definition (AMD)** and **Dependency Injection (DI)**, but they are out of the scope of this book in order to keep things simple but ready for further refinements.

Constructor functions

Constructor functions are used to define classes in our solution instead of literals. This is very important, especially for Knockout.JS ViewModels, but also for every other element that we have to handle in the presentation layer (data models, services, and so on). Object literals should only be used for simple objects setups, such as pure JSON data, but also in this case, it's a good idea to abstract its definition using a constructor function; after all, we are paid to write code.

> JavaScript is an object-oriented programming language but doesn't have a strict definition for classes as in Java or C#. Even if we can use the new operator to define an object, we have to use a function invocation after that keyword, not a real class definition.
>
> However, there are features that still remain valid in JavaScript pseudo classes, such as private members and privileged methods that are not available in the object literals.

The following is a typical class definition using a constructor function:

```
var MyClass = function () {
  var myPrivateVariable, myPrivateFunction;
  myPrivateVariable = "This is a private variable";
  myPrivateFunction = function (x) {
    return x + 1;
  };
  this.myPublicProperty = "This is a public property";
  this.myPublicMethod = function () {
    return myPrivateVariable;
  }
}
```

Using this class definition is very simple:

```
var myClassInstance = new MyClass();
var value = myClassInstance.myPublicMethod();
```

Encapsulating the data and behavior (properties and methods) in a class definition helps a lot when we have to test our solution. We can leverage object-oriented programming principles which leads to a better design, which, in turn, produces code that is easier to test. For example, if we follow the **Single Responsibility Principle**, every class will focus on a few things so that we can soon identify the correct tests to be written and will have clear dependencies, so as to create a mock-up of them and test them in isolation.

Every class should be written in its own JavaScript file. There are techniques during the build time that will concatenate and minify all of them in a single release file which will be used in production.

The module pattern

JavaScript doesn't have the concept of namespace, and furthermore, managing the global variable scoping is not easy. In a complex application using several third-party libraries and frameworks, we really need something that can be used as a sandbox to ensure the uniqueness for symbols and identifiers.

In this situation, we can use one of the most known JavaScript idiomatic patterns: the **module pattern**. This pattern is a good solution if we need to introduce a class definition sandboxing, not only to "protect" our names and signatures, but also because it's very useful when we work in a team and every member has to focus on different parts of the solution. In fact, with this kind of magic box, we can individually test our classes and be sure that they will work when we put every part together.

The module pattern is based on self-executing functions, another well-known idiomatic JavaScript syntax with several implementations, such as the following:

```
this.myModule = (function (module) {
module.MyClass = function () {
        //MyClass definition
}
return module;
}(this.myModule || {}));
```

Here's a brief explanation:

- `this.myModule` is a property assignment: `this` is the global JavaScript object (in a web browser it's the `window` object), `myModule` is the property that will contain the module definition. It's important that this identifier is as unique as possible because it will be exposed to every other library (it's our brand identifier such as `jQuery` or `ko`).

- `(function (module) {...}(...))` is a self-executing function. There is the anonymous function definition first and immediately after there is its invocation (the two outer parentheses are a common habit, placed to inform that the enclosed function is a self-executing one). The return value will be assigned to the `myModule` global property.

- `this.myModule || {}` is the argument passed to the self executing function. This is a common expression that takes into account two possible situations. If `this.myModule` has already been assigned, it will be passed to the function; otherwise, the function will receive an empty literal object, which will be the initial module object. This is considered a micro-optimization. When the global scoped objects (such as a document or window) are passed, it gives immediate scope so that the browser doesn't have to search through the scope chain.

- The self-executing function content takes the `module` object as an argument. Then, it defines some module content (in this example, we add a `MyClass` definition). Finally, it returns the module itself and this is the result that is assigned to the `myModule` global property.

If we use this module definition for every class we need to define, in every file, we can sleep easy because no matter how many times we call this assignment, no matter in which order, this idiomatic syntax will add a new piece of functionality to the module. The first time `this.myModule` will be undefined so as to start with an empty literal object, and from the second time onward we will reassign the `myModule` global object to itself, adding something new inside the self-executing function every time.

MVVM and unit testing

When we decide to use a presentation pattern as the most important pillar of a software solution, we are also establishing a specific direction to follow in developing the application.

We need to understand that if we decide to adopt Knockout.JS, it is because it grants us some important concrete advantages, not because we have to simply choose one of the many JavaScript frameworks out there.

In *Chapter 2, The Knockout.JS UI Framework Explained*, we talked about one of the advantages: a clear separation between the user interface and presentation logic. Why is this a real benefit? There are several possible answers, but if we want to remain in the unit testing context, we can apply proper unit testing specifications to the presentation logic, independent from the user interface.

In **MVVM**, the ViewModel is a pure-code representation of the View. The View itself is (must remain) a thin and simple layer, whose job is to present the data and receive the user interaction. This is a great scenario for unit testing. All the logic in the presentation layer is located in the ViewModel and this is a JavaScript object. We can definitely test almost everything that takes place in the presentation layer.

Effective separation between the View and ViewModel

Ensuring a real separation between the View and ViewModel means that we need to follow a particular development procedure:

1. Think about a web application page as a composition of subviews. We need to embrace the *divide et impera* principle when we build our user interface. The more subviews are specific and simple, the more we can test them easily. Knockout.JS supports this kind of scenario very well.

2. Write a class for every View and a corresponding class for its ViewModel. The first class is the starting point to instantiate the ViewModel and apply bindings. After all, the user interface (the HTML markup) is what the browser loads initially.

3. Keep each View class as simple as possible; so simple that it might not even need to be tested. It should just be a container for:

    °   Its ViewModel instance

    °   Sub-View instances within the View; in case of a bigger View that is a composition of smaller ones

    °   Pure user interface code; in case of particular UI JavaScript plugins that cannot take place in the ViewModel and simply provide graphical effects/enrichments (in other words, they don't change the logical functioning)

These rules are all applied in the **My Todo** sample application. Let's see all of them in detail.

The My Todo web application

First of all, we need to build the user interface. The sample application uses Bootstrap (http://getbootstrap.com/) as the main UI framework. Taking into account the UI mock-up we presented earlier in this chapter, we can generate the following HTML markup:

```html
<!DOCTYPE html>
<html lang="en">
<head>
    <meta charset="utf-8">
    <meta http-equiv="X-UA-Compatible" content="IE=edge">
    <meta name="viewport" content="width=device-width, initial-
scale=1">
    <title>My Todo</title>
    <link href="styles/smoothness/jquery-ui-1.10.4.custom.min.css"
rel="stylesheet">
    <link href="styles/bootstrap.min.css" rel="stylesheet">
    <link href="styles/app.css" rel="stylesheet">
</head>
<body>
    <div class="container">
        <nav class="navbar navbar-default" role="navigation">
            <div class="container-fluid">
                <div class="navbar-header">
                    <a class="navbar-brand" href="#">My Todo</a>
                </div>
                <div class="collapse navbar-collapse" id="bs-example-
navbar-collapse-1">
                </div>
            </div>
        </nav>
        <div class="row">
            <div class="col-md-8" id="todoListView">
                <!-- todo list content -->
            </div>
            <div class="col-md-4" id="newItemView">
                <!-- new item form content -->
            </div>
        </div>
    </div>
    <!-- javascript 3rd parties libraries script references -->
    <!-- javascript source script references -->
</body>
</html>
```

Here, we used some HTML comments as placeholders for other HTML markup to save space and show the main View structure more clearly. Note that we have identified three views (the main page and its two sections: the item list and new item form), so now we need to define their respective classes and ViewModels. It's important here to understand that the main page usually doesn't need a ViewModel. In fact, most times, the main page is nothing else than a container that doesn't have any functional part.

With unit testing in mind, we can proceed from the ground up, developing and testing the two individual components independently, and then put everything together.

The new to-do item form

The first step is to always define the UI (the following HTML markup is placed inside the `newItemView` div):

```
<div class="panel panel-default">
  <div class="panel-heading">
    <h3 class="panel-title">New ToDo Item</h3>
  </div>
  <div class="panel-body">
    <div role="form">
      <div class="form-group">
        <label for="todoItemTitle">Title</label>
        <input type="text" class="form-control" id="todoItemTitle"
placeholder="Enter Title" data-bind="value: title, valueUpdate:
'input'">
      </div>
      <div class="form-group">
        <label for="todoItemDescription">Description</label>
        <textarea class="form-control" rows="3"
id="todoItemDescription" placeholder="Enter Description" data-
bind="value: description, valueUpdate: 'input'"></textarea>
      </div>
      <div class="form-group">
        <label for="todoItemDueDate">Due Date</label>
        <input type="text" class="form-control" id="todoItemDueDate"
placeholder="Enter Due Date" data-bind="value: dueDate">
      </div>
      <button type="button" class="btn btn-primary" data-bind="click:
insertNewTodoItem, enable: canInsertNewTicket">
        <span class="glyphicon glyphicon-ok"></span>  Insert
Item
      </button>
    </div>
  </div>
</div>
```

This is a classic Bootstrap form with three input fields (title, description, and due date) and a button that the user has to click to insert a new to-do item. Note that we already defined the data-bind attributes. In this book, we don't present every example in its entirety, otherwise the book would be too long, but in real-world development, the production process is an iterative task. Usually we need to:

- Define a View markup skeleton without any data-bind attributes
- Start developing classes for the View and ViewModel, which are empty at the beginning
- Start developing the presentation logic and adding observables to the ViewModel and their respective data bindings in the View
- Start writing test specifications

This process is repetitive, adding more presentation logic at every iteration until we reach the final result.

The following is the ViewModel class:

```
this.mytodo = (function (mytodo) {
    mytodo.NewTodoItemViewModel = function (eventBus, myTodoService) {
        var self;

        self = this;

        self.title = ko.observable("");
        self.description = ko.observable("");
        self.dueDate = ko.observable("");

        self.canInsertNewTicket = ko.computed(function () {
            return self.title() && self.description() && self.
dueDate();
        });

        self.insertNewTodoItem = function () {
            var insertTodoItemSuccess, insertTodoItemError,
newTodoItem;

            newTodoItem = {
                title: self.title(),
                description: self.description(),
                dueDate: new Date(self.dueDate())
            };
```

```
            insertTodoItemSuccess = function () {
                eventBus.postNewTodoItemInserted(newTodoItem);
                self.title("");
                self.description("");
                self.dueDate("");
            };

            insertTodoItemError = function () {
                eventBus.postError("Error inserting new Todo item");
            };

            myTodoService.insertTodoItem(newTodoItem,
    insertTodoItemSuccess, insertTodoItemError);
          };
      };
    return mytodo;
} (this.mytodo || {}));
```

Let's now explain some of the concepts we used that are very important in terms of the application architecture and unit testing.

The constructor function receives two arguments:

- `eventBus` is an important application asset whose job is to ensure communication between the ViewModels and/or views using the event collaboration (we'll see more on this in the next paragraph)

- `myTodoService` is an instance of the `mytodo.MyTodoService` class; it acts as a service facade for a remote resource such as a RESTful service (more on this in a later paragraph)

These two objects are the ViewModel dependencies that can be easily mocked up when we start to write test specifications.

 In this book, we need to keep things unrelated to unit testing, simple and class dependency management is one of these. In modern web application development, there are many advanced techniques and frameworks that help managing dependencies (we have already mentioned **AMD** and **DI**), but they are out of the scope of this book, so dependencies are simply passed as arguments through the class constructor.

The View class is pretty simple:

```
this.mytodo = (function (mytodo) {
    mytodo.NewTodoItemView = function (eventBus, myTodoService) {
        var self, newTodoItemViewModel;

        self = this;
        newTodoItemViewModel = new mytodo.
NewTodoItemViewModel(eventBus, myTodoService);

        self.init = function () {
            jQuery("#todoItemDueDate").datepicker({
                changeMonth: true,
                changeYear: true,
                minDate: 1
            });
            ko.applyBindings(newTodoItemViewModel, document.
getElementById("newItemView"));
        };
    };

    return mytodo;
}(this.mytodo || {}));
```

Here, we can see that the View class receives the same two arguments passed to the ViewModel instance (and it's clear that the View has the responsibility to instantiate its ViewModel). It also exposes a public method called `init`, which activates the Knockout bindings. The class is very simple (as it should be) and contains pure UI-related code. We used a jQuery UI plugin to activate a *datepicker* in the `todoItemDueDate` input field.

Why did we decide to instantiate the ViewModel inside the View and also activate a datepicker there? The reason is always the same, separation between the View and ViewModel from the perspective of unit testing. If we look carefully at the ViewModel class implementation, we can see that there are no HTML markup references; no tag names, no tag identifiers, nothing. All of these references are present in the View class implementation. In fact, if we were to test a ViewModel that holds a direct reference to a UI item, we would also need a live instance of the UI; otherwise, accessing that item reference would cause a null reference runtime error during the test. This is not what we want because it is very difficult to test a presentation logic having to deal with a live instance of the user interface; there are many reasons for this, from the need of a web server that delivers the page to the need of a separate instance of a web browser to load the page. This is not very different from debugging a live page with **Mozilla Firebug** or **Google Chrome Developer Tools**. Our objective is test automation but we also want to run tests easily and quickly in isolation; we don't want to run the page in any way!

There is another important reason; when you work on a team or when the product requirements change frequently. The user experience experts and developers can work separately most of the time because there is only one place in which the two worlds collide, the View class. If the UI experts should decide to change the page markup, the user interface effects, and widgets, but not to alter the presentation logic, they are free to do so because they are working on a pure-UI level. The only code that the developers have to change is related to the data-bind attributes and some UI references inside the View class. For example, if they want to change the jQuery UI datepicker with another super cool Bootstrap widget, they have to change a few lines of code inside the View class, but they don't need to change anything in the ViewModel class. In this way, they can save our test specifications that remain valid over UI modifications.

The event bus

In the previous section, we talked about the event bus as an important application asset. This is a global object, which works as an event/message broker for all the actors involved in the web page (Views and ViewModels).

Event bus is one of the alternative forms of the **Event Collaboration** design pattern (http://martinfowler.com/eaaDev/EventCollaboration.html):

> *Multiple components work together by communicating with each other by sending events when their internal state changes.*
>
> *– Martin Fowler*

The main aspect of an event bus is that:

> *... the sender is just broadcasting the event, the sender does not need to know who is interested and who will respond. This loose coupling means that the sender does not have to care about responses, allowing us to add behavior by plugging new components ...*
>
> *– Martin Fowler*

In this way, we can maintain all the different components of a web page completely separated. Every View/ViewModel couple sends and receives events but they don't know anything about all the other couples. Again, every ViewModel is completely decoupled from its View (remember that the View holds a reference to the ViewModel, but not the other way around) in case it can trigger some events to communicate something to the View.

Concerning unit testing, loose coupling means that we can test our presentation logic one single component at a time, simply ensuring that the events are broadcast when they need to. Event buses can also be mocked so that we don't need to rely on a concrete implementation.

This example of an event bus class is quite simple and uses a third-party library called **Postal.JS** (`https://github.com/postaljs/postal.js`; obviously, there are other libraries you can use to achieve the same result):

```
this.mytodo = (function (mytodo) {
    var guid,
        newTodoItemInsertedEvent = "EVENT_NEW_TODO_ITEM_INSERTED",
        errorEvent = "EVENT_ERROR";

    guid = function () {
        function s4() {
            return Math.floor((1 + Math.random()) * 0x10000).
toString(16).substring(1);
        }
        return function () {
            return s4() + s4() + "-" + s4() + "-" + s4() + "-" + s4()
+ "-" + s4() + s4() + s4();
        };
    };

    mytodo.EventBus = function () {
        var self, channel;

        self = this;
        channel = postal.channel(guid());

        self.postNewTodoItemInserted = function (todoItem) {
            channel.publish(newTodoItemInsertedEvent, todoItem);
        };
        self.onNewTodoItemInserted = function (handler) {
            channel.subscribe(newTodoItemInsertedEvent, handler);
        };

        self.postError = function (message) {
            channel.publish(errorEvent, message);
        };
        self.onError = function (handler) {
            channel.subscribe(errorEvent, handler);
        };
    };
    return mytodo;
}(this.mytodo || {}));
```

Here, the behavior is quite simple. For every event, there are a couple of methods:

- A method to post the event and its data
- A method to subscribe to the event broadcast by passing a handler function

In this example, the event bus defines two main events:

- If a new to-do item inserted successfully, it broadcasts the item that was just inserted
- If an error occurs, it broadcasts the error message

For the sake of completeness, the guid method ensures that the Postal.JS channel has a unique identifier.

Managing services and third-party libraries

In a complex web application, it is quite common to use third-parties libraries and remote services. Our My Todo application in its simplicity is a perfect example in this regard. We have a remote service (usually a RESTful service), which acts as a remote end point to communicate with the server and underlying database. We also have a special object, the event bus, which acts as an event broker for the internal communication between the UI components.

These two objects share some characteristics; they are not directly related to the UI, they act as services, and their implementations require some third-party libraries. When we need to test a JavaScript web application, we want to test our code and our code only (it's quite hard to test what we produce, usually we don't have the time to worry about someone else's code…).

The objective here is to manage the third-party libraries and services in a way that will help us write test specifications, the best option we have is to encapsulate them in dedicated classes. In this way, we can create stubs/mocks to simulate and control their behavior when it's time for a test. Encapsulation also has another big advantage, our class acts as a filter for the library functionalities. In this way, we can write a specific API for our application that is simpler to use than the original and is good for unit testing.

In the previous paragraph, we saw the event bus implementation. If we look carefully at the code, we notice that it follows all the directives we just mentioned. The Postal.JS library is hidden inside our EventBus class, which, in turn, exposes a simple API that is specific to our application. For example, we hid all the string constants used by Postal.JS, exposing specific methods that speak the application language at the same time.

On the other hand, we can do the same with services; the following is the
`MyTodoService` class implementation:

```
this.mytodo = (function (mytodo) {
  var getTodoListUrl = "http://<URL_TO_SERVICE_GETTODOLIST_METHOD>",
    insertTodoItemUrl = "http://<URL_TO_SERVICE_INSERTTODOITEM_
METHOD>",
    callRestService = function (url, data, successCallback,
errorCallback) {
      jQuery.ajax({
        type: "POST",
        cache: false,
        cors: true,
        contentType: "application/json",
        url: url,
        data: JSON.stringify(data),
        dataType: "json",
        success: function (result) {
          successCallback(result);
        },
        error: function () {
          errorCallback();
        }
      });
    };

  mytodo.MyTodoService = function () {
      var self = this;

      self.getTodoList = function (successCallback, errorCallback) {
        callRestService(getTodoListUrl, null, successCallback,
errorCallback);
      };

      self.insertTodoItem = function (todoItem, successCallback,
errorCallback) {
          callRestService(insertTodoItemUrl, null, successCallback,
errorCallback);
      };
    };

  return mytodo;
}(this.mytodo || {})));
```

What's important here is that we have a class, which exposes some specific application methods (getTodoList and insertTodoItem) encapsulating the classic jQuery.ajax method at the same time to retrieve and send data to a remote RESTful service.

It is not always possible or convenient to hide a library API inside an application class, but in general, this is a good practice.

The to-do item list

The to-do item list View is nothing more than a simple HTML table:

```html
<div class="panel panel-default">
  <div class="panel-heading">
    <h3 class="panel-title">ToDo List</h3>
  </div>
  <div class="panel-body">
    <table class="table table-striped table-condensed">
      <thead>
        <tr>
          <th>Completed</th>
          <th>Title</th>
          <th>Description</th>
          <th>Due Date</th>
        </tr>
      </thead>
      <tbody data-bind="foreach: todoItems">
        <tr data-bind="css: { danger: isLate, success: done }">
          <td><input type="checkbox" data-bind="checked: done"></td>
          <td data-bind="text: title, css: { ticketDone: done }"></td>
          <td data-bind="text: description, css: { ticketDone: done
}"></td>
          <td data-bind="text: formattedDueDate, css: { ticketDone:
done }"></td>
        </tr>
      </tbody>
    </table>
  </div>
</div>
```

Notice here that the data-bind attributes define some CSS class modifications when the checkbox is checked, through the done ViewModel property. It's very important to understand that in this case, the ViewModel is a single to-do item. We are inside a foreach data bind. This means that the binding context changes, and it's related to the current observable array item in the loop.

The following is the ViewModel class:

```
this.mytodo = (function (mytodo) {
    mytodo.TodoListViewModel = function (eventBus, myTodoService) {
        var self;

        self = this;

        eventBus.onNewTodoItemInserted(function (todoItem) {
            self.todoItems.push(new mytodo.ToDoItem(todoItem));
        });

        self.todoItems = ko.observableArray([]);

        self.loadTodoList = function () {
            var loadTodoListSuccess, loadTodoListError;

            loadTodoListSuccess = function (todoItems) {
                var i;
                self.todoItems.removeAll();
                for (i = 0; i < todoItems.length; i += 1) {
                    self.todoItems.push(new mytodo.
ToDoItem(todoItems[i]));
                }
            };

            loadTodoListError = function () {
                eventBus.postError("Error loading Todo list");
            };

            myTodoService.getTodoList(loadTodoListSuccess,
loadTodoListError);
        };
    };
    return mytodo;
}(this.mytodo || {}));
```

Nothing strange here, but it's important to note that we have an event bus subscription (eventBus.onNewTodoItemInserted); we also need to show the ToDoItem class, which represents a minimal ViewModel of a single to-do item:

```
this.mytodo = (function (mytodo) {
    mytodo.ToDoItem = function (todoItem) {
        var self;

        self = this;
```

```
        self.title = ko.observable(todoItem.title);
        self.description = ko.observable(todoItem.description);
        self.dueDate = ko.observable(todoItem.dueDate);
        self.done = ko.observable(false);
        self.formattedDueDate = ko.computed(function () {
            return self.dueDate().toLocaleDateString();
        });
        self.isLate = ko.computed(function () {
            return (self.dueDate() < new Date()) && (!self.done());
        });
    };


    return mytodo;
}(this.mytodo || {}));
```

Here, we have some regular data property and two computed observables, which refine the information content (notice the done property whose value drives the CSS class applied to the HTML table row).

Every consideration that we made for the NewTodoItemViewModel class is still valid here, and the same applies to the View class:

```
this.mytodo = (function (mytodo) {
    mytodo.TodoListView= function (eventBus, myTodoService) {
        var self, todoListViewModel;

        self = this;
        todoListViewModel = new mytodo.TodoListViewModel(eventBus,
myTodoService);

        self.init = function () {
            ko.applyBindings(todoListViewModel, document.getElementByI
d("todoListView"));
            todoListViewModel.loadTodoList();
        };
    };
    return mytodo;
}(this.mytodo || {}));
```

The main page View

Once we have defined the two components of the application, we need to put everything together when the page is loaded in the browser. In the application architecture, we are proposing to implement this step using a main View that represents the whole page.

Then, we wouldn't need to have a corresponding ViewModel because the objective here is to bootstrap all the application components, not to hold some presentation logic.

The main View class is as follows:

```
this.mytodo = (function (mytodo) {
    mytodo.MyTodoView = function () {
        var self, newTodoItemView, todoListView, eventBus,
myTodoService;

        self = this;
        eventBus = new mytodo.EventBus();
        myTodoService = new mytodo.MyTodoService();
        todoListView = new mytodo.TodoListView(eventBus,
myTodoService);
        newTodoItemView = new mytodo.NewTodoItemView(eventBus,
myTodoService);

        eventBus.onError(function (message) {
            alert(message);
        });

        self.init = function () {
            todoListView.init();
            newTodoItemView.init();
        };
    };

    return mytodo;
}(this.mytodo || {}));
```

It's clear that we have globally instantiated the event bus and the application service, and then the two component views (passing the two previous services to them). We also have an `init` method that must be called to initialize the page. It's interesting that the global error handler is placed in this class. This is because we want to consolidate the error handling strategy in a single place.

The final step is to call the `init` method. The following piece of code is what we have just before the closing `body` tag in the HTML page markup (remember that we put some HTML comments to save some space when we previously showed the main page markup):

```html
<!-- javascript 3rd parties libraries script references -->
    <script type="text/javascript" src="scripts/libs/jquery-
1.11.1.min.js"></script>
    <script type="text/javascript" src="scripts/libs/jquery-ui-
1.10.4.custom.min.js"></script>
    <script type="text/javascript" src="scripts/libs/conduit-
0.3.2.min.js"></script>
    <script type="text/javascript" src="scripts/libs/lodash-2.4.1.min.
js"></script>
    <script type="text/javascript" src="scripts/libs/postal-
0.10.0.min.js"></script>
    <script type="text/javascript" src="scripts/libs/bootstrap.min.
js"></script>
    <script type="text/javascript" src="scripts/libs/knockout-
3.1.0.min.js"></script>
    <!-- javascript source script references -->
    <script type="text/javascript" src="scripts/src/EventBus.js"></
script>
    <script type="text/javascript" src="scripts/src/MyTodoService.
js"></script>
    <script type="text/javascript" src="scripts/src/TodoItem.js"></
script>
    <script type="text/javascript" src="scripts/src/TodoListViewModel.
js"></script>
    <script type="text/javascript" src="scripts/src/
NewTodoItemViewModel.js"></script>
    <script type="text/javascript" src="scripts/src/TodoListView.
js"></script>
    <script type="text/javascript" src="scripts/src/NewTodoItemView.
js"></script>
    <script type="text/javascript" src="scripts/src/MyTodoView.js"></
script>
    <script type="text/javascript">
        jQuery(document).ready(function () {
            var myTodoView = new mytodo.MyTodoView();
            myTodoView.init();
        });
    </script>
```

The page loads all the necessary JavaScript files, both third-party libraries and application sources, and then instantiates the main page View object and calls its `init` method when the HTML document is fully loaded.

Unit testing

In the previous sections, we made many important considerations about solution architecture and structure, and code implementation using design principles and patterns, keeping in mind the web application testing. Now it's time to verify how we can test our application written in this way.

In the following section, we will present a couple of examples related to the My Todo application, which are meaningful in our context. They show why we decided to follow some specific design directives.

Integration testing

External libraries encapsulation is a perfect strategy to test an application service behavior. The objective of integration testing is to verify that our class behaves correctly using the underlying third-party library.

We don't have to test that the external library works correctly, we need to verify that our service API is well designed and works properly in collaboration with the library itself. In this context, we talk about integration testing because we need to run tests using both, our code and the library. Jasmine can therefore be used not only for BDD unit testing, but also for integration testing.

An event bus is a perfect example of this kind of situation and the following is a specification test that verifies that the newly inserted to-do item works properly:

```
describe("Given an EventBus instance", function () {
    var eventBus;
    beforeEach(function () {
        eventBus = new mytodo.EventBus();
    });
    it("should call the handler when a newTodoItemInsertedEvent is
triggered", function () {
        var newTodoItem, handler;
        spyOn(eventBus, "onNewTodoItemInserted").and.callThrough();
        handler = jasmine.createSpy("handler");
        eventBus.onNewTodoItemInserted(handler);
        newTodoItem = {
            title: "Title",
            description: "Description",
            dueDate: new Date("04/06/2014")
        };
        eventBus.postNewTodoItemInserted(newTodoItem);
        expect(handler).toHaveBeenCalled();
        expect(handler.calls.count()).toEqual(1);
```

```
        expect(handler.calls.argsFor(0).length).toEqual(2);
        expect(handler.calls.argsFor(0)[0]).toEqual(newTodoItem);
    });
});
```

Here, in the `it` function, we can identify the following steps:

1. A spy object is defined on the event bus `onNewTodoItemInserted` method, which calls the real method when invoked (we need to track the real method invocations).

2. A spy object is defined, which acts as the event handler.

3. The handler created in step 2 is used to subscribe to the new to-do item insert event.

4. The event is triggered posting a new to-do item.

5. Some expectations are verified, which are as follows:

   ○ The event handler is called

   ○ The event handler is called just once

   ○ Two arguments are passed to the event handler when called (this is a specific Postal.JS API behavior)

   ○ The first argument passed to the event handler when called is the new to-do item posted when an event is triggered

This is a typical integration test, and can be usually used to verify that all the infrastructure objects work properly before performing all the other test specifications. This is because these objects will be mocked in those specifications. Their behavior is assumed to be correct when mock objects are initialized, so it's imperative to be sure that this is true; otherwise, nothing will work properly at runtime.

Use case testing

At this point in the chapter, we have all the elements to deal with the presentation logic testing. We can think about this topic as the most important objective of this book, but I don't want you to think that this is a sequential journey that leads to a specific destination. In a practical book like this one, we are almost forced to organize content in chapters and paragraphs, and although topics seem to follow a predefined sequence, real-world development shouldn't necessarily proceed this way.

There are several development methodologies strictly related to unit testing, but this book is not intended to be an **Application Lifecycle Management** (**ALM**) encyclopedic report whose objective is to teach you how to organize your delivery process.

However, at some point in time, during some kind of iteration, you may need to test your presentation logic. The best way to approach this task is to think about the use cases for at least two main reasons:

- End users use our applications because of their functionalities and we should think with their mindset and concentrate on use cases, because users are our most critical success factor
- Thinking about our applications, one use case at a time helps develop a team's schedule delivery over time, estimate efforts, milestones, and iterations more easily

In this scenario, Jasmine is the perfect unit testing framework because its BDD nature applies very well when we need to code testing that verifies use cases.

In the My Todo application, there is a use case that we can exploit as a perfect example of this approach, that is, the insertion of a new to-do item. This use case is quite simple; a user fills the new item form (title, description, and due date), clicks on the insert button in order to send the request to the remote service (the new item is added in the database on the server side) and to show the new item in the to-do item list, and finally, the new item form resets.

In the following screenshot, the user filled the **New ToDo Item** form before clicking on the **Insert Item** button:

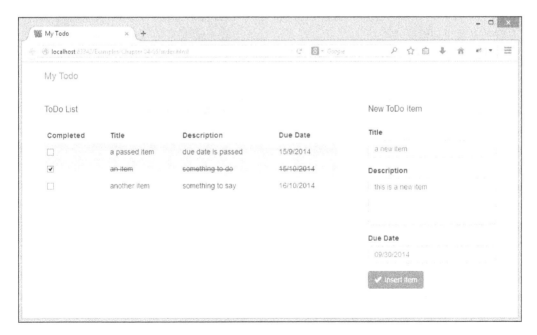

After clicking on the **Insert Item** button, the new item is inserted in **ToDo List**, as shown in the following screenshot:

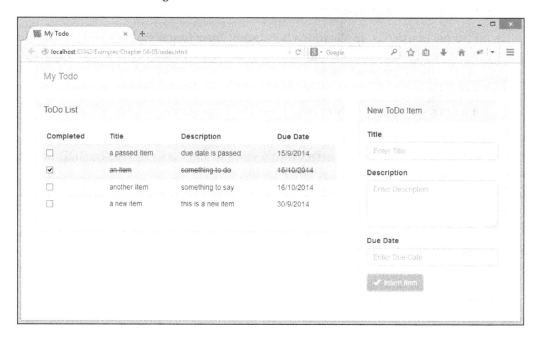

First of all we need to define the context of this specification: *given the user that wants to insert a new to-do item*:

```
describe("Given the user that wants to insert a new todo item",
function () {
    var newTodoItemViewModel, todoListViewModel, eventBus,
myTodoService, onNewTodoItemInsertedHandler;

    //context setup
    beforeEach(function () {
        //mocking eventBus and remote service
        eventBus = jasmine.createSpyObj("eventBus",
["postNewTodoItemInserted", "onNewTodoItemInserted", "postError"]);
        //faking event subscription to save event handler reference
for further use
        eventBus.onNewTodoItemInserted .and.callFake(function
(handler) {
            onNewTodoItemInsertedHandler = handler;
        });
```

```
        myTodoService = jasmine.createSpyObj("myTodoService",
["insertTodoItem"]);
        //ViewModels initializations
        newTodoItemViewModel = new mytodo.
NewTodoItemViewModel(eventBus, myTodoService);
        newTodoItemViewModel.title("Title");
        newTodoItemViewModel.description("Description");
        newTodoItemViewModel.dueDate("04/06/20014");
        todoListViewModel = new mytodo.TodoListViewModel(eventBus,
myTodoService);
        todoListViewModel.todoItems([
            new mytodo.ToDoItem({
                title: "A title",
                description: "A description",
                dueDate: new Date("02/06/2014")
            })
        ]);
        //event subscription verification
        expect(eventBus.onNewTodoItemInserted).toHaveBeenCalled();
        expect(eventBus.onNewTodoItemInserted.calls.count()).
toEqual(1);
    });
    //...
});
```

The `beforeEach` method initializes the specification context. We have defined
two mocks for the event bus and application service. We have initialized the two
ViewModels with some data because they are both involved in our use case. We also
verified that the `TodoListViewModel` instance has successfully subscribed to the event.

Now we can test the successful case (when the remote service submission works
without errors)—when a new todo item is inserted, then the form should reset,
the item remotely inserted, and the item list updated:

```
it("when a new todo item is inserted, then the form should reset, the
item remotely inserted, " +
  "and the item list updated", function () {
  var dueDate, newTodoItem;
  //mocking remote service insert method (successful)
  myTodoService.insertTodoItem.and.callFake(function (item,
successCallback, errorCallback) {
    successCallback();
  });
```

```
    dueDate = new Date(newTodoItemViewModel.dueDate());
    newTodoItem = {
      title: "Title",
      description: "Description",
      dueDate: dueDate
    };
    //item insertion
    newTodoItemViewModel.insertNewTodoItem();
    //form reset verification
    expect(newTodoItemViewModel.title()).toEqual("");
    expect(newTodoItemViewModel.description()).toEqual("");
    expect(newTodoItemViewModel.dueDate()).toEqual("");
    //remote service call verification
    expect(myTodoService.insertTodoItem).toHaveBeenCalled();
    expect(myTodoService.insertTodoItem.calls.count()).toEqual(1);
    expect(myTodoService.insertTodoItem.calls.argsFor(0).length).
toEqual(3);
    expect(myTodoService.insertTodoItem.calls.argsFor(0)[0]).
toEqual(newTodoItem);
    //event verification
    expect(eventBus.postError).not.toHaveBeenCalled();
    expect(eventBus.postNewTodoItemInserted).toHaveBeenCalled();
    expect(eventBus.postNewTodoItemInserted.calls.count()).toEqual(1);
    expect(eventBus.postNewTodoItemInserted.calls.argsFor(0).length).
toEqual(1);
    expect(eventBus.postNewTodoItemInserted.calls.argsFor(0)[0]).
toEqual(newTodoItem);
    //faking event propagation
    onNewTodoItemInsertedHandler(newTodoItem);
    //item list verification
    expect(todoListViewModel.todoItems().length).toEqual(2);
    expect(todoListViewModel.todoItems()[1]).toEqual(jasmine.any(mytodo.
ToDoItem));
    expect(todoListViewModel.todoItems()[1].title()).
toEqual(newTodoItem.title);
    expect(todoListViewModel.todoItems()[1].description()).
toEqual(newTodoItem.description);
    expect(todoListViewModel.todoItems()[1].dueDate()).
toEqual(newTodoItem.dueDate);
});
```

Here, in the `it` function, we can identify the following steps:

1. The application service mock method is faked to respond successfully.
2. The item is inserted invoking the correct ViewModel method.
3. Some expectations are verified. These are as follows:
   - The form resets
   - The application service is called properly
   - The error event is not triggered
   - The new to-do item inserted event is triggered once
4. The event propagation is forced.
5. The to-do item list is correctly updated with a new item.

Notice that we needed to force the event propagation. This is because we are not using the real event bus, but a mock. We cannot rely on the external library (Postal.JS) whose job is to notify subscribers when an event is triggered, so we need to impose the event bus behavior inside the test. This is not an integration test. We want to test our use case in isolation from every third-party library because the use case drives the entire behavior of every component involved, and not the other way around. In fact, we can say that the use case unit test should be written before anything else, using infrastructure objects as black boxes, and only then we can implement the event bus and application service in the way dictated by the use case.

Maybe now you can fully understand why the sequence of paragraphs doesn't mean a specific development process that must be followed step-by-step in the same order.

Finally, we can test the erroneous case: when a new item is inserted, and remote service throws an error, then the form doesn't reset, and an error is raised:

```
it("when a new item is inserted, and remote service throws an error,
then the form doesn't reset, " +
  "and an error is raised", function () {
  var dueDate, newTodoItem;
  //mocking remote service insert method (with error)
  myTodoService.insertTodoItem.and.callFake(function (item,
successCallback, errorCallback) {
    errorCallback("Error");
  });
  dueDate = new Date(newTodoItemViewModel.dueDate());
  newTodoItem = {
    title: "Title",
```

```
        description: "Description",
        dueDate: dueDate
    };
    //item insertion
    newTodoItemViewModel.insertNewTodoItem();
    //form verification
    expect(newTodoItemViewModel.title()).toEqual("Title");
    expect(newTodoItemViewModel.description()).toEqual("Description");
    expect(newTodoItemViewModel.dueDate()).toEqual("04/06/20014");
    //remote service call verification
    expect(myTodoService.insertTodoItem).toHaveBeenCalled();
    expect(myTodoService.insertTodoItem.calls.count()).toEqual(1);
    expect(myTodoService.insertTodoItem.calls.argsFor(0).length).
toEqual(3);
    expect(myTodoService.insertTodoItem.calls.argsFor(0)[0]).
toEqual(newTodoItem);
    //event verification
    expect(eventBus.postNewTodoItemInserted).not.toHaveBeenCalled();
    expect(eventBus.postError).toHaveBeenCalled();
    expect(eventBus.postError.calls.count()).toEqual(1);
});
```

Finally, when running all the example tests we wrote in this chapter, the result we get is the following:

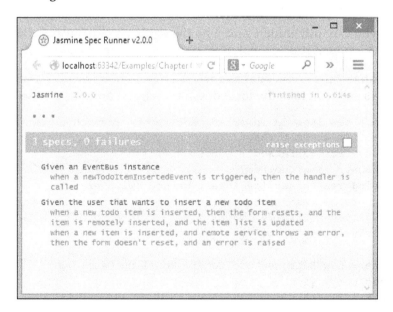

Summary

This chapter is the core of the entire book. It gives an adequate outlook about unit testing, trying to focus on topics not necessarily related to tools and frameworks but to development strategies and conceptual considerations about how we can be successful.

You learned how to structure and organize your JavaScript solution in terms of folders and files. Then, you learned how to take advantage of JavaScript idiomatic patterns to write better code, which is also easier to test.

You also learned why MVVM is a good choice if you need to test a web application extensively, and how to practically use it in the correct way having a unit test as the main development target.

Finally, you learned the difference between integration and use case testing, and separately managing View/ViewModels from services and third-party libraries.

In the next chapter, we will take a step forward towards a complete application lifecycle management. We will set up a build system to achieve unit testing automation and continuous delivery.

Setting Up an Effective Testing Environment

5

One of the most important practical aspects of unit testing is the development environment. Unit testing a web application should be as easy as possible, and this is not only a matter of application design and frameworks.

In the previous chapters, we analyzed how to properly design a web application and how to introduce unit testing effectively, yet this is not enough. We also need to put together a development pipeline that is easy to set up, organize, and run continuously. In fact, one of the most important objectives of unit testing is to have control over the development progresses, which can be better if executed at every single code modification.

We need a system focused on task automation so that we can execute our unit testing suites in a comprehensive build process, from the development source code, to the delivery production package. In this regard, there are a lot of different products and tools that we can adopt, but we will try to propose a possible solution. Generally speaking, we should always be on the alert because new products and tools are coming with better integration and productivity.

In this chapter, we will learn:

- What NodeJS is and how it helps in web development and testing
- How to automate common web development tasks using GulpJS, and how they are related to unit testing
- How to automate unit testing using Karma
- How to automate page simulation and testing using PhantomJS

The NodeJS ecosystem

The most exciting web development innovation in the last years is, without any doubt, **NodeJS**.

The best definition of NodeJS can be found on the official website of NodeJS (http://nodejs.org/):

> "**NodeJS** *is a platform built on* **Chrome's JavaScript runtime** *for easily building fast, scalable network applications.*
>
> *NodeJS uses an event-driven, non-blocking I/O model that makes it lightweight and efficient, perfect for data-intensive real-time applications that run across distributed devices.*"

This definition clearly states that NodeJS is a sort of runtime engine used to run web applications; in fact, it's mostly used as an HTTP/TCP server. But NodeJS is more than that: it has been designed in a very flexible way so that it can be used in several other contexts.

The NodeJS API is written in JavaScript, and this is one of the main advantages in terms of web development. There is another characteristic that is very important in our context: NodeJS is cross-platform (it can be easily installed on Linux, Mac, and Windows) and runs locally (via command line) on every type of computer, from big-blade servers, to regular development laptops.

NodeJS is the go-to tool to test web applications. In fact, it is not only another web container born to host our applications (such as **Microsoft IIS** or **Apache**); it is a runtime engine, so it can virtually host any kind of software.

Another great NodeJS feature is **Node Package Manager** (**npm**), a preinstalled utility that manages and organizes third-party programs and tools. Everyone can develop and distribute a NodeJS package that runs hosted inside the runtime engine and is not necessarily related to web hosting.

Third-party and built-in packages can be used in the same way, simply importing the corresponding reference inside a NodeJS program. For example, if we want to run the HTTP web server, we need to import the specific built-in package. A simple NodeJS program file (called http_server.js) can be as follows:

```
var http = require("http");
http.createServer(function (req, res) {
  res.writeHead(200, {"Content-Type": "text/plain"});
  res.end("Hello World\n");
}).listen(8080, "127.0.0.1");
```

At first, we import the `http` package and create the server on `localhost`, port number 8080 (`http://127.0.0.1:8080`). To run the server hosted in NodeJS, we simply have to open the command line and execute the command (`node http_server.js`), which invokes the `node` executable and passes the startup file as an argument. Have a look at the following screenshot:

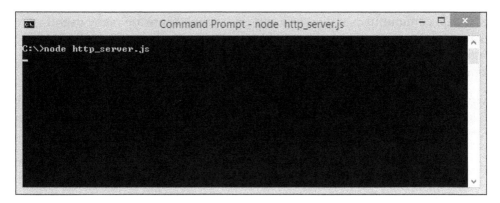

We can then test the web server by simply making a GET request (command prompt must remain up and running, otherwise, NodeJS runtime stops, and so will the web server). Have a look at the following screenshot:

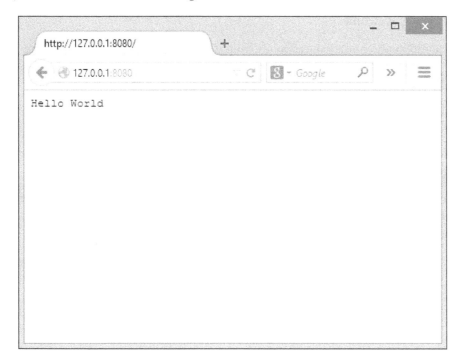

The same principles apply to other tools that we want to run hosted in NodeJS:

- Install them with **npm** as a third-party package
- Write a JavaScript startup file
- Run NodeJS by pointing at the main file

The NodeJS community is very active and productive: there are many useful packages we can use in our daily web development activities. In the following paragraphs, we will describe some of them that will help us in unit testing automation and solution delivery.

Obviously, there are other products that we can use for the same purposes, usually well integrated in most known IDEs (such as JetBrains Webstorm), but I think there are at least three good reasons to choose NodeJS:

- NodeJS is multiplatform: it can be used in any development environment without any changes
- NodeJS is built on V8, the most popular JavaScript runtime, designed by web developers for web developers; nothing else can be more web oriented
- NodeJS is very efficient, scalable, and fast in terms of execution performance

Still, if you want to use NodeJS as the fastest and scalable web server available today, you are clearly welcome.

Task automation with GulpJS

Before talking about unit testing automation (that is the main objective of this chapter), we need to introduce another concept: task automation.

What do we really mean by the term *task automation*? Well, we need to talk about what we need to do when delivering a web application to production.

The one and only true objective of web development is to publish a fully functioning and optimized web application. In this regard, there are several well-known best practices that have to be respected, at least:

- **Source code quality verification**: Using tools like **JSLint** or **JSHint**, we need to check the quality of our source code in search of possible style convention deficiencies as well as structural problems

- **Source file concatenation**: We need to build a unique source code file in order to include a single `script` tag in the corresponding web page (remember that every script tag is a call to the web server, thus a delay in the page load process; it's important to reduce as much as possible every call)

- **Source code minification**: We need to reduce the source code file dimension as much as possible in order to reduce the script download time from the web server, for example, removing all unnecessary characters such as spaces and new lines, and renaming variables, thereby shortening their identifier, without changing any functionality

We can talk about a sort of build process even if this is technically different from a classical build process (JavaScript is an interpreted language, we don't need to create a binary executable, but these transformations helps a lot when we need to publish our solution).

The previous points are, however, strictly related to web application testing: code quality verification, source file concatenation and source code minification usually change the original source code (especially minification), which is the one we wrote and tested. Consequently, we need to re-execute all the test suites over the source code resulting from the build process: we need to assure that all the tests pass before publishing the final web application version.

Try to imagine a regular, day-by-day development process: we make some modification to the source code to add some new features; we write and execute some new tests; then we publish the new version when everything is correct and complete. Maybe our development methodology is agile-related: we add small modifications at every short iteration, so we need to repeat the complete lifecycle, from code modification to publication, many times. In this context, we really need something that helps us in the build process: repetitive tasks that don't need direct user interaction should be automated and executed continuously with minimal effort.

GulpJS (`http://gulpjs.com/`) is one of the emerging tools to achieve task automation.

GulpJS is a NodeJS package that acts as a build system, and its core responsibility is to co-ordinate and run single, specific tasks over an initial configuration. Every different type of task is in turn a particular GulpJS plugin. Dozens of plugins are available from the GulpJS website (`http://gulpjs.com/plugins/`): not only CSS compilation, JavaScript minification, images thumbnail creation, but also version control systems integration, and many others.

There are other build systems built on NodeJS, such as **GruntJS** (`http://gruntjs.com`), probably the most adopted as of now, but I think GulpJS is the easiest to use.

JSLint and unit testing

Why use a code quality tool when we are trying to verify our applications through unit testing? This is a good question that hides a misunderstanding.

JavaScript was born as a simple programming language to perform tiny operations in a web page. **Douglas Crockford**, in his book, *JavaScript: The Good Parts*, states:

> *"JavaScript is built on some very good ideas and a few very bad ones.*
>
> *The very good ideas include functions, loose typing, dynamic objects, and an expressive object literal notation. The bad ideas include a programming model based on global variables."*

In this book, he dedicates two full appendices to the *Awful* and *Bad* parts of the language (not only global variables), but another one is used to introduce **JSLint** (http://www.jslint.com/), a code quality tool for JavaScript:

> *"It (JSLint) takes a source text and scans it. If it finds a problem, it returns a message describing the problem and an approximate location within the source. The problem is not necessarily a syntax error, although it often is. JSLint looks at some style conventions as well as structural problems. It does not prove that your program is correct. It just provides another set of eyes to help spot problems.*
>
> *JavaScript is a sloppy language, but inside it there is an elegant, better language. JSLint helps you to program in that better language and to avoid most of the slop."*

Before writing and running tests, it's very important to write solid JavaScript code following some well-known code conventions that can dramatically reduce errors upfront.

Unit testing and code quality verification are two different aspects of the same process: writing better code, code that works as expected.

A code quality tool, such as JSLint, is something like a watchdog; sometimes it can be annoying because it follows some code conventions that can be too strict, but in general they save you from the typical JavaScript bad habits. For example, JSLint considers the unary operators ++ and -- too tricky and subject to security menaces, so it doesn't permit their use.

In general, every code quality tool comes with configuration options so that we can reduce their rigidity and customize how they work, but I suggest that you don't change anything and learn how they want you to write good JavaScript.

The build system installation

Installing the GulpJS build system is an easy procedure. First, we need NodeJS to be installed; this is as simple as running its installer that we can find on NodeJS website. Then, we simply need to run the following **npm** commands from the command line, starting from a local `build` folder (generally, I prefer to place this folder inside the project's `script` folder at the same level as that of `libs`, `src`, and `tests` folders):

```
npm install -g gulp

npm install gulp --save-dev

npm install gulp-concat --save-dev

npm install gulp-uglify --save-dev

npm install gulp-jslint --save-dev
```

The first line installs GulpJS globally (the `-g` option) in the system; this is needed because we will run GulpJS on the NodeJS command line. Then, the second line installs all of the GulpJS development dependencies (the `--save-dev` option). From the third to the last line, it installs the three GulpJS plugins we need (file concatenation, source code minification, JSLint code quality verification) and their development dependencies. It's very important not to forget to install all the development dependencies because they play a primary role during development and testing. Differently from GulpJS package, the three plugins are installed locally in the `build` folder under a special `node_modules` subfolder automatically created by npm.

The build system configuration

After the installation, we need to configure our build process: GulpJS is configured by writing a special file called `gulpfile.js`, which is placed in the `build` folder. The upcoming code is a simple configuration file that doesn't contain any test automation task (we will dig into test automation in the next paragraph).

Have a look at the following code:

```
/*global console*/

var gulp = require("gulp");

var concat = require("gulp-concat");
var jsLint = require("gulp-jslint");
var uglify = require("gulp-uglify");

var jsLintOptions = {
    browser: true,
    white: true,
    predef: ["jQuery", "JSON", "ko", "require", "postal", "alert"],
    sloppy: true,
    unparam: true,
    reporter: "default",
    errorsOnly: true
};

var paths = {
    src: [
        "../src/*.js"
    ]
};

gulp.task("release", function () {
    return gulp.src(paths.src)
        .pipe(concat("mytodo.min.js"))
        .pipe(uglify())
        .pipe(gulp.dest(".."));
});
gulp.task("debug", function () {
    return gulp.src(paths.src)
```

```
            .pipe(jsLint(jsLintOptions));
});

gulp.task("build", [
    "debug",
    "release"
]);

gulp.task("default", ["build"]);
```

The configuration file starts with four variable declarations: they contain the main GulpJS reference and the three plugins references using the `require` statement (we are loading all the needed tools).

In the `jsLintOptions` variable, we define all the analysis options for JSLint, in particular, the `reporter` option set to `default` means that JSLint will output its messages in the regular command-line flow.

In the `path` variable, we define all the source code files we want to consider, which, in this case, are all the files inside the `src` folder (using the `*.js` notation, they will be used in alphabetical order; if you need a different ordering you have to write every file in the order you want inside the `src` array).

Then, we define two GulpJS tasks: `release` and `debug`. A task is basically a stream of files a series of sequential operations is applied to. For example, in the `release` task, first we target the file stream using the `gulp.src` function over the `path.src` set of files; then, we apply the concatenation (specifying the resulting file name) and minification sequentially using the `gulp.pipe` function; and then the final resulting file (`mytodo.min.js`) is created in the parent folder using the `gulp.dest` function.

As a general rule, several `gulp.pipe` invocations define the set of operations applied over the `gulp.src` set of source files.

The `debug` task only applies JSLint (with its configuration options) on the source code files; we don't apply code quality verification in the `release` task because we only need to verify the original source code once.

At the end, we define a third task called `build` that is the concatenation of the `debug` and `release` tasks.

Finally, we define the main default task, that is, the one GulpJS runs if no task are specified at runtime, which in this case is the `build` task.

To execute GulpJS with this configuration, you simply need to run the shell command line pointing to the build folder and then run the `gulp` command, as shown in the following screenshot:

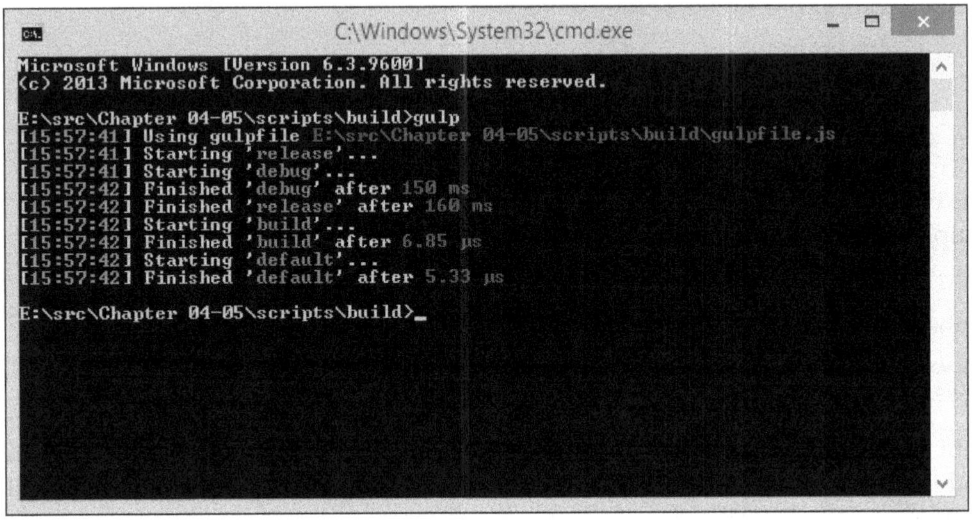

In the case of an error during the build procedure, the process stops, and the error is reported in the command-line messages, for example, the JSLint error shown in the following screenshot:

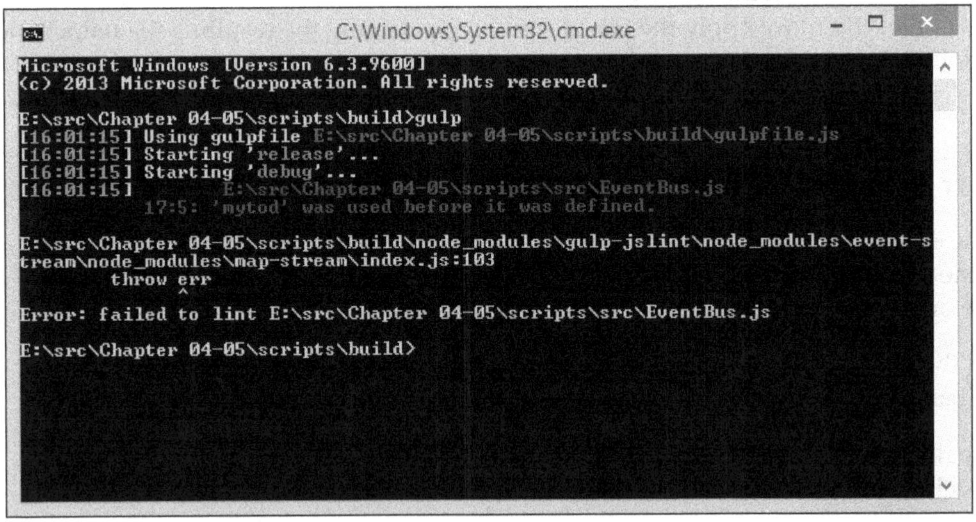

Once the build process has created the `mytodo.min.js` file, we can run our application in production, modifying the script references. The original HTML markup fragment inside the `index.html` page is as follows:

```html
<!-- src -->
<script type="text/javascript" src="scripts/src/EventBus.js"></script>
<script type="text/javascript" src="scripts/src/MyTodoService.js"></script>
<script type="text/javascript" src="scripts/src/TodoItem.js"></script>
<script type="text/javascript" src="scripts/src/TodoListViewModel.js"></script>
<script type="text/javascript" src="scripts/src/NewTodoItemViewModel.js"></script>
<script type="text/javascript" src="scripts/src/TodoListView.js"></script>
<script type="text/javascript" src="scripts/src/NewTodoItemView.js"></script>
<script type="text/javascript" src="scripts/src/MyTodoView.js"></script>
<script type="text/javascript">
  jQuery(document).ready(function () {
    var myTodoView = new mytodo.MyTodoView();
    myTodoView.init();
  });
</script>
```

Every single source code file is referenced in a dedicated `script` tag; we can use this version when debugging or developing the application. In production, we can use the following release version:

```html
<!-- src -->
<script type="text/javascript" src="scripts/mytodo.min.js"></script>
<script type="text/javascript">
  jQuery(document).ready(function () {
    var myTodoView = new mytodo.MyTodoView();
    myTodoView.init();
  });
</script>
```

The debug version is very useful if you need to debug your running web page step-by-step using the browser developer tool (for example **Firefox Firebug**). The release version is not human readable because it's minified, but it's good for the production environment because its size is the smallest possible.

Unit testing automation with Karma (in GulpJS)

In the previous paragraph, we set up a build process the main objective of which is to verify our code quality and create a release version of the source code. At this point, we need to complete this process introducing unit testing.

One of the most important GulpJS plugins is the **Karma** integration. Karma (`http://karma-runner.github.io/`) is a testing environment that provides a series of useful features for developers, such as:

- It runs tests on different kinds of browsers (not only different vendors, but also devices, such as phones and tablets) or using a **PhantomJS** instance

- It supports a series of unit testing frameworks, such as **Jasmine**, **QUnit**, and **Mocha**

- It can be integrated in several development environments, such as IDEs and browsers, for example, **Jetbrains Webstorm** or **Google Chrome Developer Tools**

- It can be integrated into several continuous integration systems, for example, **Jenkins**, **Travis**, or **Semaphore**

The first two features are the most important because Karma gives us the freedom to choose the unit testing framework we prefer (Jasmine in this case) and because using PhantomJS, we can run the test suites on real browsers and devices automatically (we will cover PhantomJS in the next section).

The testing environment installation

Installing Karma as a GulpJS plugin is quite easy, we just need to add the following commands to the previous build system installation:

```
npm install -g karma-cli
npm install karma --save-dev
npm install karma-jasmine@2_0 --save-dev
npm install karma-phantomjs-launcher --save-dev
npm install karma-html-reporter --save-dev
npm install gulp-karma --save-dev
```

First, we install the Karma command line globally; then, we locally install the main Karma runtime engine, the Jasmine integration for Karma, the PhantomJS launcher, a Karma plugin that creates unit testing reports in the Jasmine style automatically, and finally the GulpJS plugin for Karma.

The testing environment configuration

To configure all the build processes with unit testing, we first need two additional configuration files: the Karma configuration files for *debug* and *release* placed in the same `build` folder of `gulpfile.js`.

The `karma.debug.js` configuration file is as follows:

```
module.exports = function (config) {
    config.set({
        basePath: "",
        frameworks: ["jasmine"],
        reporters: ["progress", "html"],
        htmlReporter: {
            outputDir: "../tests/reports/debug",
            templatePath: __dirname + "/node_modules/karma-html-
reporter/jasmine_template.html"
        },
        browsers: ["PhantomJS"],
        port: 9878,
        colors: true,
        logLevel: config.LOG_INFO,
        singleRun: true
    });
};
```

In this file, we set some Karma options:

- The empty base path means the `build` folder
- Jasmine as unit test framework
- Two kinds of reporters: the default one that writes messages in the command-line flow, and the HTML reporter that creates HTML report pages in the Jasmine style
- The HTML reporter configuration (we simply specify where to write the reports and where to find the page template)
- PhantomJS as the browser to use
- The HTTP port to use for PhantomJS
- Other miscellaneous options (colored output, log level, and single run)

The following `karma.release.js` configuration file is very similar:

```
module.exports = function (config) {
    config.set({
        basePath: "",
        frameworks: ["jasmine"],
        reporters: ["progress", "html"],
        htmlReporter: {
            outputDir: "../tests/reports/release",
            templatePath: __dirname + "/node_modules/karma-html-
reporter/jasmine_template.html"
        },
        browsers: ["PhantomJS"],
        port: 9877,
        colors: true,
        logLevel: config.LOG_INFO,
        singleRun: true
    });
};
```

In this file, we simply changed where to create the HTML report, and the HTTP port for PhantomJS (we need another port; otherwise the two configurations will conflict).

We also need to modify the GulpJS configuration in the following way:

```
var gulp = require("gulp");

var concat = require("gulp-concat");
var jsLint = require("gulp-jslint");
var uglify = require("gulp-uglify");
var karma = require("gulp-karma");

var jsLintOptions = {
    browser: true,
    white: true,
    predef: ["jQuery", "JSON", "ko", "require", "postal", "alert"],
    sloppy: true,
    unparam: true,
    reporter: "default",
    errorsOnly: true
};
```

```
var paths = {
    src: [
        "../src/*.js"
    ],
    testsRelease: [
        "../libs/jquery-1.11.1.min.js",
        "../libs/jquery-ui-1.10.4.custom.min.js",
        "../libs/conduit-0.3.2.min.js",
        "../libs/lodash-2.4.1.min.js",
        "../libs/postal-0.10.0.min.js",
        "../libs/bootstrap.min.js",
        "../libs/knockout-3.1.0.min.js",
        "../mytodo.min.js",
        "../tests/*_Specs.js"
    ],
    testsDebug: [
        "../libs/jquery-1.11.1.min.js",
        "../libs/jquery-ui-1.10.4.custom.min.js",
        "../libs/conduit-0.3.2.min.js",
        "../libs/lodash-2.4.1.min.js",
        "../libs/postal-0.10.0.min.js",
        "../libs/bootstrap.min.js",
        "../libs/knockout-3.1.0.min.js",
        "../src/*.js",
        "../tests/*_Specs.js"
    ]
};

gulp.task("release", function () {
    return gulp.src(paths.src)
        .pipe(concat("mytodo.min.js"))
        .pipe(uglify())
        .pipe(gulp.dest(".."));
});

gulp.task("debug", function () {
    return gulp.src(paths.src)
        .pipe(jsLint(jsLintOptions));
});
```

```
gulp.task("testsRelease", function () {
    return gulp.src(paths.testsRelease)
        .pipe(karma({
            configFile: "karma.release.js",
            action: "run"
        }));
});

gulp.task("testsDebug", function () {
    return gulp.src(paths.testsDebug)
        .pipe(karma({
            configFile: "karma.debug.js",
            action: "run"
        }));
});

gulp.task("build", [
    "debug",
    "testsDebug",
    "release",
    "testsRelease"
]);

gulp.task("default", ["build"]);
```

In this new `gulpfile.js` configuration, we can find the following:

- The reference for the Karma plugin using the `require` statement.

- Two new path references, `testsDebug` and `testsRelease`, that identify all the files involved in Jasmine unit testing. In fact, we can find all the third-party libraries in the correct order, the source code, and the specification files (`../tests/*_Specs.js`). Note that in the debug path, there is a reference to the original source code files (`../src/*.js`), while in the release path there is a reference to the `mytodo.min.js` minified file.

- Two new tasks, `testsDebug` and `testsRelease`, that simply run unit tests with Karma using the corresponding paths and Karma configuration files.

- The `build` task now also includes the two new tasks.

What we are doing here is running unit tests during the build process using the same third-party libraries and the same unit test specifications, but different source code: the original source code in the debug version, and the minified source code in the release version. We can summarize the build process this way:

- The `debug` task: original source code quality verification with JSLint

- The `testsDebug` task: unit tests with Jasmine using the original source code

- The `release` task: original source code concatenation and minification to produce the optimized production code

- The `testsRelease` task: unit tests with Jasmine using the production code

Basically, we set up a build strategy that controls our code first with JSLint, then with unit tests, and then again with unit tests on the production code (I want you to remember that it's very important to run unit tests on minified code as well).

We can run the build process in the same way using the `gulp` command in the shell command line, as shown in the following code:

```
C:\Windows\System32\cmd.exe                                    _  □  ×

Microsoft Windows [Version 6.3.9600]
(c) 2013 Microsoft Corporation. All rights reserved.

E:\src\Chapter 04-05\scripts\build>gulp
[16:31:39] Using gulpfile E:\src\Chapter 04-05\scripts\build\gulpfile.js
[16:31:39] Starting 'coverage'...
[16:31:39] Starting 'debug'...
[16:31:39] Starting 'testsDebug'...
[16:31:39] Starting 'release'...
[16:31:39] Starting 'testsRelease'...
[16:31:39] Finished 'debug' after 165 ms
[16:31:39] Finished 'release' after 151 ms
[16:31:39] Starting Karma server...
[16:31:39] Starting Karma server...
[16:31:39] Finished 'coverage' after 189 ms
INFO [karma]: Karma v0.12.23 server started at http://localhost:9877/
INFO [karma]: Karma v0.12.23 server started at http://localhost:9878/
INFO [launcher]: Starting browser PhantomJS
INFO [launcher]: Starting browser PhantomJS
INFO [PhantomJS 1.9.7 (Windows 8)]: Connected on socket gpdJdiUlJjnlbyvy0vPy wit
h id 31762255
INFO [PhantomJS 1.9.7 (Windows 8)]: Connected on socket soSLnFZOD-4uET1g0vPy wit
h id 20760803
PhantomJS 1.9.7 (Windows 8): Executed 5 of 5 SUCCESS (0 secs / 0.007 secs)
PhantomJS 1.9.7 (Windows 8): Executed 5 of 5 SUCCESS (0.006 secs / 0.008 secs)
[16:31:43] Finished 'testsRelease' after 3.85 s
[16:31:43] Finished 'testsDebug' after 3.91 s
[16:31:43] Starting 'build'...
[16:31:43] Finished 'build' after 8.37 µs
[16:31:43] Starting 'default'...
[16:31:43] Finished 'default' after 6.85 µs

E:\src\Chapter 04-05\scripts\build>
```

This is what we get if a specification that doesn't pass:

We have to admit that this is not a good unit test report; it's very hard to read and understand what's going on here. That is why we also use an HTML reporter. We can find the HTML unit test reports in the tests\reports\debug and tests\reports\release folders. Opening the index.html page, we can see a typical Jasmine report.

The following screenshot shows a successful case:

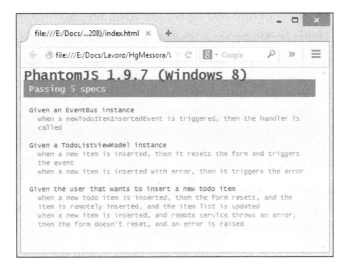

The following screenshot is the result of an error:

The command-line report is usually just a unit test semaphore: if something goes wrong we can see some red error messages. Then we can dig into the problem using the HTML report. If everything is good, we don't need to do anything (all the tests are certainly green).

Code coverage

Another important aspect of unit testing is code coverage. According to Wikipedia
(http://en.wikipedia.org/wiki/Code_coverage):

> *"In computer science, code coverage is a measure used to describe the degree to which the source code of a program is tested by a particular test suite. A program with high code coverage has been more thoroughly tested and has a lower chance of containing software bugs than a program with low code coverage. Many different metrics can be used to calculate code coverage; some of the most basic are the percent of program subroutines and the percent of program statements called during execution of the test suite."*

Karma has a code coverage plugin using **Istanbul** (http://gotwarlost.github.io/istanbul/) integration. Istanbul is a great code coverage tool, written in JavaScript and with an outstanding HTML report.

Code coverage installation is very easy; we just need to add the following npm invocation to the build system installation:

```
npm install karma-coverage --save-dev
```

Its configuration is also very easy; we don't need to change anything in the GulpJS configuration. We just need to apply a simple modification to the karma.debug.js configuration file (code coverage is an analysis tool: we only need to analyze the original source code and not the production one). Have a look at the following code:

```
module.exports = function (config) {
    config.set({
        basePath: "",
        frameworks: ["jasmine"],
        reporters: ["progress", "html", "coverage"],
        htmlReporter: {
            outputDir: "../tests/reports/debug",
            templatePath: __dirname + "/node_modules/karma-html-
reporter/jasmine_template.html"
        },
        preprocessors: {
            "../src/*.js": ["coverage"]
        },
        coverageReporter: {
            type: "html",
```

```
            dir: "../tests/coverage/"
        },
        browsers: ["PhantomJS"],
        port: 9878,
        colors: true,
        logLevel: config.LOG_INFO,
        singleRun: true
    });
};
```

In this Karma configuration file, we can see a new `coverage` entry in the `reporters` option, and then two new options:

- `preprocessors`: Identifies the source code files to analyze
- `coverageReporter`: Identifies where to create the coverage HTML report

Running the build process using GulpJS, we won't see any difference in the shell, but we will obtain the code coverage report in the `tests\coverage` folder. This report is very detailed, and we can dig into every single source code file to verify which statements are covered by unit tests and which aren't (outlined in red) in terms of the percentage of covered statements, branches, functions, and lines. The first report page is shown in the following screenshot:

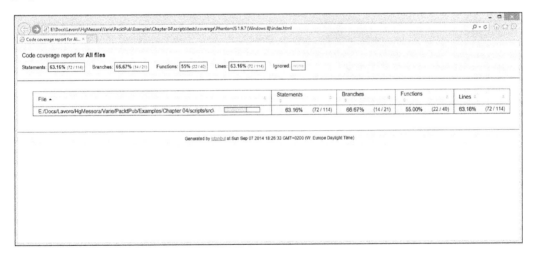

The following screenshot is the overall source file report. We can see the coverage percentage in terms of statements, branches, functions, and lines of code:

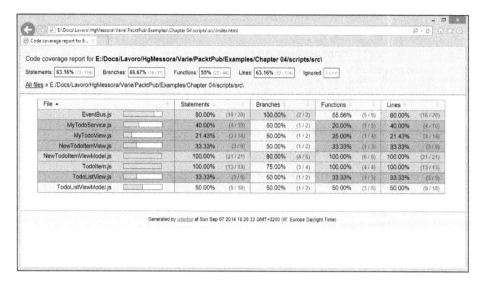

A single source file report is shown in the following screenshot. We can see the lines of code not covered by any test highlighted in red:

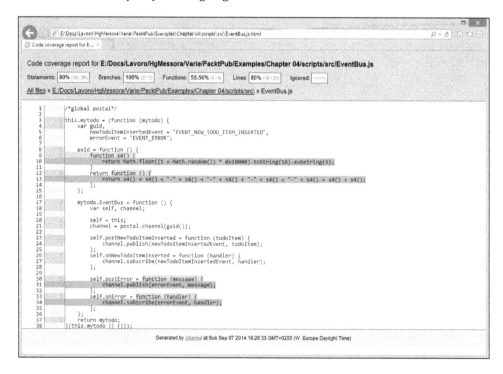

User interface testing with PhantomJS

Introducing Karma, we talked about PhantomJS and its usage as a virtual browser during unit testing execution. More precisely, PhantomJS (http://phantomjs.org/) is a headless WebKit scriptable browser, which means that:

- It's based on the well-known WebKit web engine
- It downloads a web page from a URL, renders the content into the DOM, executes JavaScript if present, and the executed result will be reflected on the browser's DOM
- It doesn't render the page into a visualized content
- The term scriptable means that we can instrument a PhantomJS instance to do actions using a JavaScript API

PhantomJS is not related in any way to NodeJS and its plugin ecosystem: it's a simple cross-platform executable (can be installed on Windows, Mac, and Linux) that runs independently from other runtime engines.

Most common PhantomJS uses are (from PhantomJS website):

- **Headless web testing**: Run functional tests with frameworks such as Jasmine
- **Screen capture**: Programmatically capture web content, including SVG and Canvas, and create website screenshots with thumbnail preview
- **Page automation**: Access and manipulate web pages with the standard DOM API or with usual libraries like jQuery
- **Network monitoring**: Monitor page loading

Headless web testing is what we do in our build system using Karma, but another interesting feature is page automation. Page automation can be used to set up a different type of web testing: user interface testing.

Once we have installed PhantomJS, we can run a user interface test using an automation script with its JavaScript API. For example, a simple use case can be expressed with the following code:

```
console.log("Given the user that wants to insert a new todo item, when
a new todo item is inserted, " +
    "then the form resets, and the item is remotely inserted, and the
item list is updated.");
var page = require("webpage").create();
page.open("http://localhost/Examples/Chapter%2004/index.html",
function(status) {
```

```
        if (status !== "success") {
            console.log("Unable to access network");
        } else {
            var ua = page.evaluate(function() {
                var initialTodoItemsCount = jQuery("#todoListView tbody
tr").toArray().length;
                jQuery("#todoItemTitle").val("Title").change();
            jQuery("#todoItemDescription").val("Description").change();
                jQuery("#todoItemDueDate").datepicker("setDate",
"06/06/2014").change();
                if (jQuery("#newItemView button").is(":disabled")) {
                    return "ERROR: new item button is disabled";
                }
                jQuery("#newItemView button").click();
                if (jQuery("#todoItemTitle").val() ||
jQuery("#todoItemDescription").val() ||
                    jQuery("#todoItemDueDate").datepicker("getDate")) {
                    return "ERROR: form not reset, " +
jQuery("#todoItemTitle").text();
                }
                if (!jQuery("#newItemView button").is(":disabled")) {
                    return "ERROR: new item button is still enabled";
                }
                if (jQuery("#todoListView tbody tr").toArray().length !==
(initialTodoItemsCount + 1)) {
                    return "ERROR: new item not in list";
                }
                return "SUCCESS";
            });
            console.log(ua);
        }
    phantom.exit();
});
```

This simple script can be placed in the `tests` folder in the `UseCases_
PageAutomation.js` file. It first creates a PhantomJS page object (using the
`require("webpage").create()` statement) and then tries to open the web
application's main page (with `page.open`). If the page loads successfully,
we can execute some actions on the page simulating a user interaction.

In fact, the function passed as an argument to the `page.evaluate` method contains all the code necessary to replicate one of the application use cases with jQuery:

- Count the actual to-do items in the table
- Set the title, description, and due date input boxes
- Verify that the submit button is not disabled; otherwise, return an error
- Invoke the click event on the submit button to insert a new to-do item
- Verify that the title, description, and due date input boxes are empty; otherwise, return an error
- Verify that the submit button is disabled; otherwise, return an error
- Verify that the to-do item table contains one more item; otherwise, return an error

Finally, `phantom.exit` closes the script and the PhantomJS runtime. We need the command line to execute the script from the `tests` folder:

```
phantomjs UseCases_PageAutomation.js
```

Running this command, we obtain the result shown in the following screenshot:

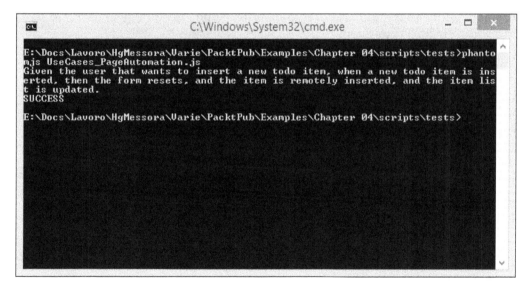

Summary

This last chapter is very important because it gives an interesting outlook on the development activities we face day-to-day. It's very important to learn and understand what unit testing is, but it's also essential to find a way to integrate all the specification suites in the complete development life cycle.

You learned what NodeJS and its ecosystem are, and how they can help in web development and testing.

Then, you learned how to set up a simple build system using GulpJS, a NodeJS Module, and automating common web development tasks, such as code quality verification and minification.

We also learned how to integrate unit testing in the build system using Karma, executing all the specification suites, including code coverage with Istanbul, during the build process.

We finally learned how to set up page automation using PhantomJS to execute user interface testing.

In this book, we covered many aspects of web application testing, not only from a technical point of view, but also in a broader development strategy in trying to set up a complete delivery system.

We have simply scratched the surface of this complex topic, there are many other topics to be addressed, and there's a lot more to say in every chapter if we wanted to dig into advanced features. For example, it's worth trying to adapt the development process to a full Test Driven Development approach. We can also try to replace Knockout.JS with another presentation framework, such as Angular.JS, because its role in the unit testing strategy would be exactly the same — only technicalities change. Finally, we can dig into the GulpJS and Karma plugins to enrich the build system with other useful delivery tasks.

Index

T

task automation, with GulpJS
  about 110, 111
  best practices 110
  build system configuration 114-117
  build system installation 113
  JSLint 112
  unit testing 112
Test Driven Development (TDD) 9, 56, 75
testsDebug task 123
testsRelease task 123
text and appearance bindings
  about 37
  attr 37
  css 37
  html 37
  style 37
  text 37
  visible 37
text binding 37
this.myModule 81
this.myModule || {} 81
ToDoItem class 93
Travis 118

U

Underscore.JS 40
uniqueName bindings 48
unit testing
  about 9, 97
  integration testing 97, 98
  use case testing 98-104
unit testing automation, with Karma
  about 118
  code coverage 126-128
  environment configuration, testing 119-125
  environment installation, testing 118
unit testing, Jasmine 55, 56
update function
  allBindings argument 52
  bindingContext argument 52
  element argument 52
  valueAccessor argument 52
  viewModel argument 52

use case testing 98-104
user interface testing, with
    PhantomJS 129-131
user stories 56

V

value binding
  about 47
  afterkeydown 47
  input 47
  keypress 47
  keyup 47
var self = this expression 34
VideModel 25
View 25, 82
View class 87
ViewModel
  about 31, 32, 82
  computed observables 33, 34
  observable arrays 34, 35
  observables 32
virtual bindings 44-46
visible binding 37

W

web resource
  about 12
  data 12
  user interface graphic styles 12
  user interface programs and executables 12
  user interface structures 12
with binding 38
World Wide Web 12

Y

Yahoo Developer Network
  reference link 24

Thank you for buying
Web App Testing Using Knockout.JS

About Packt Publishing

Packt, pronounced 'packed', published its first book *"Mastering phpMyAdmin for Effective MySQL Management"* in April 2004 and subsequently continued to specialize in publishing highly focused books on specific technologies and solutions.

Our books and publications share the experiences of your fellow IT professionals in adapting and customizing today's systems, applications, and frameworks. Our solution based books give you the knowledge and power to customize the software and technologies you're using to get the job done. Packt books are more specific and less general than the IT books you have seen in the past. Our unique business model allows us to bring you more focused information, giving you more of what you need to know, and less of what you don't.

Packt is a modern, yet unique publishing company, which focuses on producing quality, cutting-edge books for communities of developers, administrators, and newbies alike. For more information, please visit our website: www.packtpub.com.

About Packt Open Source

In 2010, Packt launched two new brands, Packt Open Source and Packt Enterprise, in order to continue its focus on specialization. This book is part of the Packt Open Source brand, home to books published on software built around Open Source licenses, and offering information to anybody from advanced developers to budding web designers. The Open Source brand also runs Packt's Open Source Royalty Scheme, by which Packt gives a royalty to each Open Source project about whose software a book is sold.

Writing for Packt

We welcome all inquiries from people who are interested in authoring. Book proposals should be sent to author@packtpub.com. If your book idea is still at an early stage and you would like to discuss it first before writing a formal book proposal, contact us; one of our commissioning editors will get in touch with you.

We're not just looking for published authors; if you have strong technical skills but no writing experience, our experienced editors can help you develop a writing career, or simply get some additional reward for your expertise.

Application Testing with Capybara

ISBN: 978-1-78328-125-1   Paperback: 104 pages

Confidently implement automated tests for web applications using Capybara

1. Learn everything to become super productive with this highly acclaimed test automation library.

2. Using some advanced features, turn yourself into a Capybara ninja!

3. Packed with practical examples and easy-to-follow sample mark-up and test code.

HTML5 Enterprise Application Development

ISBN: 978-1-84968-568-9   Paperback: 332 pages

A step-by-step practical introduction to HTML5 through the building of a real-world application, including common development practices

1. Learn the most useful HTML5 features by developing a real-world application.

2. Detailed solutions to most common problems presented in an enterprise application development.

3. Discover the most up-to-date development tips, tendencies, and trending libraries and tools.

Please check **www.PacktPub.com** for information on our titles

Web Penetration Testing with Kali Linux

ISBN: 978-1-78216-316-9   Paperback: 342 pages

A practical guide to implementing penetration testing strategies on websites, web applications, and standard web protocols with Kali Linux

1. Learn key reconnaissance concepts needed as a penetration tester.

2. Attack and exploit key features, authentication, and sessions on web applications.

3. Learn how to protect systems, write reports, and sell web penetration testing services.

KnockoutJS Starter

ISBN: 978-1-78216-114-1   Paperback: 50 pages

Learn how to knock out your next app in no time with KnockoutJS

1. Learn something new in an Instant! A short, fast, focused guide delivering immediate results.

2. Learn how to develop a deployable app as the author walks you through each step.

3. Understand how to customize and extend KnockoutJS to take your app to the next level.

Please check **www.PacktPub.com** for information on our titles

www.ingramcontent.com/pod-product-compliance
Lightning Source LLC
Chambersburg PA
CBHW060146060326
40690CB00018B/3999